T0341675

# FRENCH SCIENTIFIC AND CULTURAL DIPLOMACY

# French Scientific and Cultural Diplomacy

*Philippe Lane*

LIVERPOOL UNIVERSITY PRESS

First published as *Présence française dans le monde: L'action culturelle et scientifique* by La Documentation Française.

© 2013 Liverpool University Press

This edition published in 2013 by
Liverpool University Press
4 Cambridge Street
Liverpool
L69 7ZU

British Library Cataloguing-in-Publication data
A British Library CIP record is available

ISBN 978-1-84631-865-8 limp

Typeset by Carnegie Book Production, Lancaster
Printed and bound by CPI Group (UK) Ltd, Croydon CR0 4YY

# Contents

# List of Tables

# List of Abbreviations

| | |
|---|---|
| *Adit* | *Agence pour la diffusion de l'information technologique* |
| AEF | *Audiovisuel extérieur de la France* |
| AEFE | *Agence pour l'enseignement du français à l'étranger* |
| *Aeres* | *Agence d'évaluation de la recherche et de l'enseignement supérieur* |
| AFD | *Agence française de développement* |
| AIRD | *Agence inter-établissements de recherche pour le développement* |
| ANR | *Agence Nationale de la Recherche* |
| *Arcus* | *Action en région de coopération universitaire et scientifique* |
| Asbu | Arab States Broadcasting Union |
| AUF | *Agence universitaire de la francophonie* |
| *Belc* | *Bureau pour l'enseignement de la langue et de la civilisation françaises à l'étranger* |
| *Bief* | *Bureau international de l'édition française* |
| CCIP | *Chambre de commerce et d'industrie de Paris* |
| CFCE | *Centre français du commerce extérieur* |
| *Cicid* | *Comité interministériel de la coopération internationale et du développement* |
| *Ciep* | *Centre international d'études pédagogiques* |
| *Cirad* | *Centre de coopération internationale en recherche agronomique pour le développement* |
| CNAP | *Centre National des Arts Plastiques* |
| CNC | *Centre national du cinéma et de l'image animée* |

CNCD      *Commission nationale de la coopération décentralisée*
Cnes      *Centre national d'études spatiales*
CNL       *Centre national du livre*
Cnous     *Centre national des œuvres universitaires et scolaires*
CNRS      *Centre national de la recherche scientifique*
Cofecub   *Comité français d'évaluation de la coopération univer-*
          *sitaire et scientifique avec le Brésil*
Copeam    *Conférence permanente de l'audiovisuel méditerranéen*
CPU       *Conférence des présidents d'universités*
DAECT     *Délégation pour l'action extérieure des collectivités*
          *territoriales*
Dalf      *Diplôme approfondi de langue française*
Delf      *Diplôme d'études en langue française*
DFP       *Diplôme de français Professionnel*
DGLFLF    *Délégation générale à la langue française et aux langues*
          *de France*
DGM       *Direction générale de la mondialisation, du*
          *développement et des partenariats*
DGRCST    *Direction générale des relations culturelles, scientifiques*
          *et techniques*
DUs       *Diplômes d'université*
Ecos      *Évaluation et orientation de la coopération scientifique*
Edocdev   *L'écrit et l'accès documentaire au service du développement*
ENPI      European Neighbourhood and Partnership Instrument
ENSAD     *École Nationale Supérieure des Arts Décoratifs*
Epic      *Établissement public à caractère industriel et commercial*
Era-Net   European Research Area Network
ERDF      European Regional Development Fund
ESF       European Social Fund
EUNIC     European Union National Institutes for Culture
Fiac      *Foire internationale de l'art contemporain*
FIPF      *Fédération internationale des professeurs de français*
FPRD      Framework Programme for Research and Development
FSP       *Fonds de solidarité prioritaire*
GMES      Global Monitoring for Environment and Security

| iAOOS | Integrated Arctic Ocean Observing System |
| *Ifre* | *Instituts français de recherche à l'étranger* |
| IN2P3 | *Institut national de physique nucléaire et de physique des particules* |
| INC | *Institut de chimie* |
| INEE | *Institut écologie et environnement* |
| INP | *Institut de physique* |
| INS2I | *Institut des sciences informatiques et de leurs interactions* |
| INSB | *Institut des sciences biologiques* |
| INSH | *Institut des sciences humaines* |
| *Insis* | *Institut des sciences de l'ingénierie et des systèmes* |
| *Insmi* | *Institut national des sciences mathématiques et de leurs interactions* |
| *Insu* | *Institut national des sciences de l'univers* |
| IRD | *Institut de recherche pour le développement* |
| OECD | Organisation for Economic Co-operation and Development |
| OIF | *Organisation internationale de la francophonie* |
| OMD | *Objectifs du millénaire pour le développement* |
| PAP | *Programme d'aide à la publication* |
| PCRD | *Programme-Cadre de l'union pour la recherche et développement* |
| PHC | *Partenariats Hubert Curien* [Hubert-Curien partnerships] |
| *Pres* | *Pôles de recherche et d'enseignement supérieur* |
| R&TDFP | Research and Technology Development Framework Programme |
| RFI | *Radio France Internationale* |
| RGPP | *Révision générale des politiques publiques* |
| *Sacem* | *Société des auteurs compositeurs et éditeurs de musique* |
| *Scac* | *Service de coopération et d'action culturelle* |
| *Sofe* | *Service des œuvres françaises à l'étranger* |
| TCF | *Test de connaissance du français* |
| TEF | *Test d'évaluation de français* |
| *Umifre* | *Unités mixtes-institut de recherche à l'étranger* |
| *Valease* | *Valorisation de l'écrit en Asie du Sud-Est* |
| ZSP | *Zone de solidarité prioritaire* |

# Acknowledgements

I would like to thank His Excellency Maurice Gourdault-Montagne, Ambassador for France to Germany, Bernard Emie, Ambassador for France to the United Kingdom, Caroline Dumas, Ambassador for France to Jordan.

Thanks are also due to my colleagues in the scientific and cultural service as well as to those from the Institut Français, especially Ambassadors Xavier Darcos and Laurence Auer, for their advice and encouragement. Thanks also to Cafer Özkul, Vice Chancellor of Rouen University, Bill Burgwinkle, Conrad Smith, Máire Cross and Charles Forsdick.

I would also like to thank my contacts at the French Ministry of Foreign and European Affairs and at the other ministries promoting cultural and scientific activities outside France, not forgetting my colleagues and friends from the cultural and scientific communities.

I am very grateful to my wife Roberte, and our children, Clarin, Hugo and Tom.

# Foreword

Laurent Fabius

France as a power has influence, one of the few countries significant in world affairs. This derives from membership of the Security Council, economic and military strength, a diplomatic network, avowed universal principles, a willingness to argue beyond the country's own interests, and the language. Philippe Lane's book explores critical components of this influence in culture, the arts, academia and science.

This influence has global competition. All countries, both established and emerging powers, appreciate the strategic nature of culture, science and education for their development. From an economic perspective, these elements have their attraction: politically, they are means to exert influence.

In a competitive world, France is determined to promote its strengths. There is a readiness to build on French history, on research which is among the most innovative in the world, on the university system, and on French artists. There exists a network of influence: cultural, educational, scientific and academic cooperation unsurpassed in the world: the legacy of a long tradition of cultural and scientific outreach beyond the borders of France. The strategy is one of active influence through cooperation and cultural initiatives by embassies and by branches of the *Institut Français* and the *Alliances Françaises*.

As visiting professor in the Department of French Studies at the University of Cambridge and attaché for higher education at the French embassy in London, Philippe Lane has a thorough understanding of the diplomacy of influence. From his experience within this network, he describes French initiatives in the fields of cultural diplomacy and science. The work shows, and this is particularly striking to me personally, that this diplomacy of influence is inseparable from the advancement of empowerment, justice and progress long championed by France.

Laurent Fabius
*Minister for Foreign Affairs*

# Foreword

Sir Vernon Ellis

France and the United Kingdom are two countries with great histories; histories that include a high degree of mutual admiration and collaboration as well as the odd occasion in the past when the concepts of neighbourliness and friendship may not have been as high on our shared agendas as they fortunately are today.

Our shared histories bring many similarities to our shared present. Both countries have exercised considerable power and influence over the development of what has become the current world order; and both find ourselves less influential than we have been in the past. We are relatively small countries, after all. Nevertheless, our influence remains enormous; with our economies and international trading links playing their part, supported by an experienced and expert network of diplomacy, and the professionalism of a military presence able to contribute to the resolution of some of the more serious challenges of our time.

If these – economics and trade; diplomacy; military – are the traditional platform for a strong presence in the world, both of our countries recognise that contemporary realities require a different and additional approach.

A tradition of 'hard power' is being replaced by a focus on new concepts. Public diplomacy and cultural diplomacy, and the newer terms of 'soft power' and 'smart power' are all reflections of a recognition that influence can no longer be secured by the effective management of government-to-government relations alone, and by successful participation in the governance of international institutions – important though these are and will continue to be. Rather, in a globalised world where communications are fast and becoming faster, where the information people receive comes through media and the digital idiom, where transport and travel are easier than our forebears could ever have considered possible, in this world new approaches are required.

In the British Council we are happy to talk of "cultural relations". We like the concept of building relationships in the fields in which we work. Good relationships are based on things like friendship, mutual understanding and admiration, and on shared benefit; cultural relations are no different. This means that while we are an organisation that aims to secure benefit for our own country, the way in which we do so is firmly based on pursuing benefit for all.

As we refine our strategies in Education, English language teaching, in the Arts, we reflect on terms like "attractiveness" and "generosity". Part of our brief is to ensure that we play to the United Kingdom's strengths, to support and deploy abroad the very best that our country has to offer; all of that is to promote the attractiveness of our country. But we need to do so in a way that is generous: we need to be sensitive to what peoples overseas want from us, and not simply give what happens to suit us best. Generosity, like friendship, is based on "mutuality", another term we use when we reflect on our mission and the way we work. Where what we do is of recognised benefit to both sides, to ourselves as well as to our partners and clients in our host countries around the world, we believe we are at our most successful.

We are fortunate that the English language has developed the importance it has. This brings with it a certain responsibility; to help those who request our help in teaching and learning it. We are also fortunate we have such excellence in our universities, and the British Council provides advice and assistance to those who wish to come and study in our country. Educational links at school level remain an essential part of sensitising young people to other cultures and experiences; and perhaps nowhere more than between us and France have we achieved so much in this area. British arts justifiably have a world-class reputation, and we help our new and emerging talent find new audiences in other countries, as well as helping to build professional networks of mutual support.

The recent creation of the Institut Français in Paris with the remit of coordinating the work of some 150 institutes around the world is something we in the British Council welcome most warmly. There is already a good track record of active collaboration between us around the world, both through European institutions such as EUNIC (the grouping of the EU national institutes for culture), as well as bilateral and multilateral initiatives in individual countries. There are times when by working together we are stronger together.

This book makes a valuable contribution to the continuing conversation we are all having on the role and value of cultural relations. In the British Council, we look forward to remaining active participants in that conversation, with our colleagues in the Institut Français and our friends around the world.

Sir Vernon Ellis
*Chair of the British Council*

# Foreword

Xavier Darcos

There is more to the influence of a country than the strength of its economy, its strategic and military power and its place in the world institutions of governance. One must also consider how seductive are its ideas, its knowledge and its culture, and their relationship with the other factors of power.

Some would argue strongly that France is now in decline, with a weakening of its influence abroad. Such debates are often heated and sharply contested. The reality is more complex. The international influence of France is not in accord with its economic or demographic weight. Of course, new countries emerge on the international scene, themselves motivated by a just desire for international recognition and attraction, so crucial in the competition encountered in a divided world. Fully engaged in this competition, France enjoys a unique position the international community has always recognized.

This *smart power*, a new evolution of the *soft power* concept, is recognized as a power attribute of growing importance, and the foreign cultural and scientific policies of France are at the heart of its strategies to maintain influence around the world.

With the founding on 1 January 2011 of the *Institut français*, France has gained a new impetus to its foreign cultural policy. Succeeding, among others, to the *Cultures France* association, this new state organization was given a broader remit: to the dissemination and promotion of artistic exchanges were added the distribution of books, support for media resource centres and the French film industry, and the promotion of French thought and scientific knowledge, with help for French teaching – and training for those involved in this process.

The *Institut français*, a dedicated body answerable to the Ministry of Foreign Affairs, has a foreign cultural remit in the coordination of over 150 French Institutes throughout the world. It heads a network to unify action, crucial at a time of state budget reductions. The *Institut français* is developing a 'single denomination' policy similar to what has been the case for the British Council and the Goethe Institute over recent decades.

First through an initiative, shared with French schools abroad and the *Alliances françaises*, there is the promotion and diffusion of French, the second foreign language taught throughout the world after English – the only two languages used on every continent. France, as home to this language, wishes for there to be a link between all the countries sharing French. The language counts 116 million learners, one million of them in the Institutes and *Alliances françaises*. The promotion of the French language will gel with the other activities, the main thread being the expansion of a network of teachers and students.

This new policy of promoting artistic exchanges and collaborating with developing countries, is to be carried forward in partnership with French institutions and facilitators of cooperation abroad: *Unifrance* and the *Centre national du cinéma et de l'image animée* (CNC) for the film industry; the *Centre national du livre* and the *Bureau international de l'édition française* (*Bief*) for book publishing; together with the French regional and local authorities and the principal state cultural organizations. Of particular attractiveness are its publications and that French intellectuals, researchers and other experts can take part in debates on issues crucial to the future of society in individual countries as well as throughout international society in general.

The *Institut français*, active in science and higher education, maintains a brief for the dissemination of knowledge which drives its promotion of publishing, translation and support for media centres. This is essentially a France which debates vigorously the role of intellectual creativity: the country is high on the list for registering patents and publishing scientific articles. It also ranks third in the world for the number of foreign students it hosts.

The globalization of knowledge started a new competition and demands renewed efforts. From China to India by way of the Arab world and Latin America, new powers influence the agenda of ideas and reinforce their acceptance in science and higher education. In this context, France offers 'open diplomacy', able to project its approaches, its ideas, its methods beyond its frontiers. The promotion of scientific culture is a new priority: a programme for the diffusion of scientific culture was launched in 2011 to stimulate reflection and scientific exchange.

The reform of cultural diplomacy is a considerable undertaking and this is just the beginning. This book is a very useful contribution to clarifying the stakes and identifying the major players, and through the clarity of its analysis and its pedagogical approach it will be of interest to a wide audience.

Xavier Darcos
*Ambassadeur chargé de la politique culturelle extérieure,*
*Président de l'Institut français*

# Introduction

A philosopher must undertake three journeys: first the encyclo-
paedic journey, second a journey around the world (a philosopher
who would not have seen the oceans, the poles and the equator
would ignore the world). The third journey is one amongst
mankind ... This third journey goes two ways: one has to have
friends everywhere, have talks with all, and one has to journey
within the various social classes.

(Interview with Michel Serres, June 2003)

French cultural and scientific initiatives are very topical, judging by
the number of parliamentary reports and studies, as well as recent
announcements by government on their organization and future.

## Reports and Opinions on the Foreign Activities
## of the French Government

During the last decade or so, several parliamentary reports have
highlighted the themes of French cultural and scientific influence, from
Patrick Bloche, *Le désir de France: la présence internationale de la France
et la francophonie dans la société de l'information: rapport au Premier
ministre* (1999)[1] to François Rochebloine and Geneviève Colot, *Rapport
d'information sur 'le rayonnement de la France par l'enseignement et la
culture'* (2010).[2]

[1] <www.ladocumentationfrancaise.fr/rapports-publics/994000906/index.shtml>.
[2] <www.assemblee-nationale.fr/13/rap-info/i2506.asp>.

In addition, there have been a number of reports and opinions of non-parliamentary origin on the subject. If we add to this the numerous articles and features published in the press over recent years, we see some measure of the importance of France's cultural and scientific message, as well as the contours of its foreign cultural and scientific policies.

## New Public Institutions
## Contributing to the Foreign Initiatives of France

The law of 27 July 2010 dealing with the foreign activities of the state led to the development of new tools to renew the diplomacy and influence of France; first, from 1 January 2011, is the *Institut français*, presided over by Xavier Darcos, ambassador for the foreign cultural policies of France, the object of which is to create an integrated body to oversee the network of cultural centres and Institutes abroad.

The implementation order creating the *Institut français* was made on 30 December 2010, allowing for the new structure to replace the association *Cultures France* from 1 January 2011. During a hearing of the foreign affairs committee of the *Assemblée nationale*, Xavier Darcos reaffirmed the founding principles of this public institution: to offer to each country a nominated representative and a brand representing France through a local institute, bringing together the staff of advisers and attachés,[3] together with the staffs of existing Institutes. Thirteen countries piloted this from 2011: Cambodia, Chile, Denmark, Georgia, Ghana, India, Kuwait, Senegal, Serbia, Singapore, Syria, the United Arab Emirates and the United Kingdom, with the first *Instituts français* to be created as soon as 2012.

It is indeed a question of professionalizing the cultural network by improving training, favouring dialogue and information, developing best practice for management control and the evaluation of cooperative action, and by working more closely with French local and regional authorities and the European Union. This was to be implemented in cooperation with the Ministry for Culture and Communication.

Other than the *Institut français*, the law of 27 July 2010 also heralded the creation of a state institution, *Campus France*, under the supervision of both the Ministry for Higher Education and Research and the Ministry

---

[3] This does not apply to advisers or attachés in science or technology.

for European and Foreign Affairs. It was to take care of promoting and improving the status abroad of the French systems of higher education, research and professional training, the reception of foreign students and researchers, the management of grants, internships and other international exchange programmes, as well as the international promotion and development of higher education and research.

Finally, the law created a new public institution with an industrial and commercial vocation named *France Expertise Internationale*, supervised by the Ministry for European and Foreign Affairs and charged with the promotion abroad of French technical assistance and expertise.

Thus, even if grants devoted to cultural influence are down by 10 per cent in recent years, it becomes all the more important to ensure better collaboration between the ministries concerned on the one hand, and the cultural and scientific institutions on the other. These elements of supervision are not without importance since they have an influence on the cultural and scientific spheres, where funding and modes of cooperation with large French and foreign institutions are concerned.

We shall borrow an expression of Julia Kristeva-Joyaux's,[4] which François Roche and Bernard Pigniau[5] had already used in 1995: the problem is to escape from this bureaucratic mountain in which cultural and scientific institutions and organizations operate with no overall global cohesion. These new agencies were required to strike up new partnerships, so as to contribute to a redefinition of global political management. If in 2010 the French senate's committee for cultural affairs failed to establish a new state secretariat for foreign cultural activities, including foreign audiovisual interests and the promotion of the French language, the step forward was taken in 2011 with the creation of these agencies to guide and implement cultural and scientific policies, receiving, to take the example of the *Institut français*, up to €43 million over three years: more than the budget for the former association.

---

[4] Julia Kristeva-Joyaux, *Le message culturel de la France et la vocation interculturelle de la francophonie: Avis présenté par Mme Julia Kristeva-Joyaux*, 'Avis et rapports du conseil économique, social et environnemental'(2009) <www.enssib.fr/bibliotheque-numerique/document-40675>.

[5] François Roche and Bernard Pigniau, *Histoires de diplomatie culturelle des origines à 1995*, Ministère des affaires étrangères, Association pour la diffusion de la pensée française (ADPF) (1995).

## From Cultural Influence to a Diplomacy of Influence

A diplomacy of influence[6] differs from cultural influence in that it covers a broader field of action in the new logistics of globalization, and emphasizes the place of culture and science in the global stakes of international cooperation in such things as health, climate, migration, the regulation of financial markets, food security and education. This is what Anne Gazeau-Secret, former director general of international cooperation and development with the French European and Foreign Affairs Ministry, means when she writes:

> Cultural exchanges, artistic creativity, public debates, the French language, university and scientific cooperation, education of the high flyers, innovative projects, expertise missions, programmes of invitations to France, audiovisual cooperation, book policies: the tools which the network can and must use are varied and numerous. However, we must be wary of restricting ourselves to considering only traditional activities based upon a narrow concept of culture or to just language courses, and we must provide the means to adapt to the new order of global stakes.[7]

This is how programmes of the *Fonds d'Alembert*,[8] for instance, approach global questions such as the cultural and scientific dimensions of development.

Scientific and cultural cooperation is linked closely to the global issues of today. In 2011, the French presidency of the G20 and G8 was due to deal with the world financial system after the crisis following the fall of the bankers Lehman Brothers in 2008, illustrating how difficult it is for countries to resist a wave of protectionism and to develop world trade, the problems many countries encounter as they emerge from crisis and the strengthening of the major international financial institutions. Reforming the international monetary system, stabilizing the prices of raw materials (especially in agriculture and energy) and improving global

[6] See Anne Gazeau-Secret, 'Pour un "soft power" à la française: du rayonnement culturel à la diplomatie d'influence', *L'ENA hors les murs*, 399 (March 2010), pp. 9–12.

[7] Anne Gazeau-Secret, '(Re)-donner à notre pays sa juste place dans le monde ...', *Défense*, 140 (July–August 2009), pp. 19–21. See also Dominique Wolton, *L'autre mondialisation*, new edn. (Paris: Flammarion, 2010).

[8] See below, Chapter 4, 'Book Publishing Policy: The Debate of Ideas, Science and Knowledge'.

governance were the three priorities defined by the French president. This adds to concerns tackled already at previous summits, such as sustainable development, the social consequences of globalization and climate change. These issues are not divorced from cultural or scientific activities in that they are subjects of much ideological debate in those countries concerned by one or other of the challenges.

It follows that cultural and scientific questions are deeply interwoven with major global issues, and French foreign cultural and scientific initiatives must seek to integrate more fully these new challenges which go beyond the artistic and the linguistic.

It is vital that France should offer a revised concept of culture and science in its approach to the more general framework of a diplomacy of influence. And this is the task of the *Direction générale de la mondialisation, du développement et des partenariats* (DGM), the emphasis being on the global issues of the day, whereby cultural and scientific approaches are reconfigured to be more interdisciplinary and cross-sector, combining forces such as business and French regional and local authorities.

This need to extend the concept of culture into today's world challenges is ever more vital since the fall of the Soviet bloc after 1989, attacks on the World Trade Center in 2001 and fallout from the recent events of the 'Arab Spring'.

**Foreign Cultural and Scientific Activities: A Current Debate**

In an article appearing exclusively in *Le Monde* on 7 July 2010, '*Cessez d'affaiblir le Quai d'Orsay!*' [Stop weakening foreign affairs], two former French foreign affairs ministers, Alain Juppé and Hubert Védrine, expressed concern over the consequences for France of budget cuts in the Foreign Office, saying 'the investment-to-efficiency ratio for this modest budget is outstanding: permanent representations, embassies, consulates, *lycées*, primary schools, cultural centres, programmes of assistance and cooperation'. It follows that France must develop both the agencies and the operators in charge of cultural and scientific influence and at the same time maintain an adequate functioning and investment budget for the ministerial institutions promoting the policies of influence, such as foreign affairs, culture and communication, higher education and research.

In November 2007, *Time Magazine* reopened the debate on the world decline of French culture and language,[9] and, more recently, in its 15 July 2010 issue, *Le Nouvel Economiste* published an article by Emmanuel Lemieux on the decline of French cultural influence in the world entitled *'Nouvelle guerre coloniale, la France aurait-elle perdu la guerre du soft power?'* [Would France have lost the new colonial soft power war?][10] This was a wake-up call to stimulate and renew French cultural and scientific partnerships. How was this to be achieved? Very likely, by exploring new means of dissemination and cooperation, by adapting to the very diverse expectations of widely differing audiences, and, most importantly, by considering interculturality and a form of relativism which takes measure of the needs and wishes of the people concerned. In this way, the general review of public policies – *révision générale des politiques publiques* (RGPP) – could be an exercise in budgetary virtue that would lead to rethinking the priorities and practicalities of cultural and scientific initiatives. Choosing a strategic political management function undertaken by the ministries and operators linked to the services in the embassies implies a need for additional funding.

This present volume aims to discuss the main problems, institutions and strategies of French cultural and scientific initiatives, and at the same time to underline the vital importance of this political commitment for France, which must, in times of straitened finances, promote ever stronger and innovative partnerships in their aims, content and methods of financing.[11]

---

[9] Donald Morrison, 'In Search of Lost Time' *Time Magazine*, 21 November 2007.

[10] See also Frédéric Martel, *Mainstream: enquête sur cette culture qui plaît à tout le monde* (Paris: Flammarion, 2010), and Olivier Poivre d'Arvor, *Bug made in France, ou l'histoire d'une capitulation culturelle* (Paris: Gallimard, 2011).

[11] <www.diplomatie.gouv.fr/politique-etrangere-de-la-France/diplomatie-economique-901/>.

# 1

# French Foreign Cultural Activities:
# A Tradition with a Long History

French cultural diplomacy can trace its roots to the *Ancien Régime*,[1] since which time the links between literature and diplomacy have been extremely strong. From the sixteenth century to the eighteenth century, as Jean-François de Raymond points out in his book *L'action culturelle extérieure de la France* (2000), many diplomats were also men of letters.[2]

## Arts, Literature and Diplomacy under the *Ancien Regime*

Joachim du Bellay, famed for his collection of poems entitled *Regrets* and his *Défense et illustration de la langue française*, travelled to Rome in 1553 as secretary and steward to his powerful cousin Cardinal Jean du Bellay, who was attached to the Vatican. Thus the dual presence of the name of du Bellay, in the realm of 'letters' and in that of 'affairs' and as society dignitaries, implies that the *literary* glory attached to the name of an author cannot be distinguished readily from the *social*, where accident of birth and accomplishments at war or in politics are elements.

During this same sixteenth century, when the challenge was to protect Christians within the Ottoman Empire, François I obtained recognition from Suleiman the Magnificent that French culture and language must be preserved. French diplomacy thus defended the status of Christians to

---

[1] On all historical aspects, reference should be made to François Roche and Bernard Pigniau, *Histoires de diplomatie culturelle des origines à 1995*, Ministère des affaires étrangères, Association pour la diffusion de la pensée française (ADPF) (1995).

[2] Jean-François de Raymond, *L'action culturelle extérieure de la France* (Paris: La Documentation française, 2000).

whom this sultan had granted protection in the East in a treaty signed in 1535 with François I – the treaty on which was based the development of French cultural and linguistic influence in this part of the world. In the reign of Louis XIII, in the seventeenth century, similar examples occurred in Canada, in Madagascar, Tunis and Algiers, and through the activities of the *Société des missions étrangères* (Foreign Missionary Society) in the Far East.

This strong relationship between political and cultural activities is thus an essential part of French diplomacy: as early as the seventeenth century, Richelieu, and after him Mazarin, would appoint literary academics as ambassadors in charge of the promotion of the French language, which was the language of European courts and of the arts, and they performed an integral part in locating and securing works of art for the royal collections. In this way, the sciences, arts and literature were prerequisites to diplomatic relations and facilitated preliminary exchanges in any subsequent negotiations.

Many works linked to the functions of ambassador published in the seventeenth and eighteenth centuries highlight the cultural expertise essential to the profession of diplomat. As Jean-François de Raymond emphasizes, the rich history of scientists and artists sojourning in European courts reflects the reputation of a French presence, particularly from the sixteenth century to the eighteenth century:

> Thus Queen Christina of Sweden, who wanted to turn Stockholm into a new Athens, invited to her court, where French was spoken, painters, medal makers, poets, scientists, before herself writing political and philosophical thoughts in French. [...] In the last third of the eighteenth century, young Gustav III of Sweden, who corresponded with Louis XVI, had a monument erected in Stockholm [...] in honour of Descartes, whom d'Alembert imagined meeting with Queen Christina in the Champs Elysées, while Voltaire praised Queen Louise-Ulrika, mother of this young prince, who honoured the French language.[3]

This influence of French culture and language existed in Europe, in North Africa, in the East and the Far East, but also in North America, from the St Lawrence River to Louisiana and the Pacific coast.

---

[3] Ibid., p. 17.

The Age of Enlightenment is a good demonstration of this. As Roche and Pigniau remark,

> in the Age of Enlightenment, those whom one could have pointed out as the first 'cultural advisers' to the European courts seemed to act more in their own interests than on those of the French government. Diderot in Russia, with Catherine II, Voltaire at the court of Prussia, an influential counsellor of Frederic, are but the better known of a group of French engineers, scientists, experts, architects and artists at work throughout Europe. [...] The reality is more complex, since the authorities in France knew how to use these intellectuals to conduct more subtle, occasionally secret, diplomacy. In 1743, Voltaire travelled to The Hague to seek information on the manoeuvres of Frederic in Holland, and Beaumarchais went to London to observe public reaction to the events in America. Finally Mirabeau, three years before the French Revolution, pursued diplomacy in Prussia parallel to that of the official minister, Count d'Esterno.[4]

In 1743, Jean-Jacques Rousseau secured from M. de Montaigu the post of secretary to the embassy in Venice. But the most remarkable of the men of letters acting as diplomats was Cardinal de Bernis. A Church official and protégé of Madame de Pompadour, De Bernis was Louis XV's Minister of Foreign Affairs, a cardinal, the archbishop of Albi in southern France, and then ambassador to Rome.

At the time, arts and literature were associated with exchanges, political contacts, life in European courts and the preparation of treaties: culture and diplomacy already had strong connections. The eighteenth century essentially founded the cultural and scientific activities of France throughout the world: the evolution of mankind is nurtured by such intellectual, scientific and cultural exchanges between nations.

The profusion of revolutionary ideas would have a particular resonance in the French *Declaration of the Rights of Man and the Citizen* in 1789.

## 1789 to 1870: The Nation and Cultural Activities

The French Revolution attempted to 'nationalize' foreign cultural initiatives, according to Albert Salon:

---

[4] Roche and Pigniau, *Histoires*, p. 11.

during the last decade of the eighteenth century, all of the intellectual, diplomatic and military forces joined together to spread the new ideas of the Revolution. This evangelism and sense of mission corresponded with the voluntarism of the spirit of the Enlightenment: it was a drive for the moral and intellectual perfecting of mankind. This belief in a never-ending progress of knowledge, this strong desire to develop ideas in every sphere belongs to the dominant philosophy of the eighteenth century.[5]

This international activity also counted on the religious congregations abroad, particularly from 1789 to the period of the Restoration. For example, as a direct consequence of François I's policy, in 1801, Napoleon signed a renewal of the agreement with the Ottoman Empire for the protection of Christians in the East. His 1798 expedition to Egypt had included several scientists, engineers, intellectuals and artists who would contribute to the creation of Egyptology and to the cultural and scientific relations to follow.

For all of the nineteenth century, cultural activities continued to accompany diplomacy. This depended somewhat on the evolution abroad of religious groups. In 1882, Chateaubriand, as Minister of Foreign Affairs, demanded an increase to the meagre budget allocated to 'religious help'. Later, Guizot would grant subsidies to explorers in Tunisia with a view to supplementing the collections of the Louvre Museum. The Ministry of Foreign Affairs also followed the recommendations of Lamartine, who would be in charge at the beginning of 1848, to provide study grants in Lebanon.

During this period, the Ministry of Foreign Affairs had its diplomats negotiate the first cultural agreements, which were mainly concerned with intellectual and artistic property. Two years before the end of the Second Empire, the Galatasaray *lycée* was opened in Istanbul, a cooperative project between France and the Ottoman government. It would educate generations of French speakers who would constitute the Turkish elite in the years to follow.[6]

---

[5] Albert Salon, 'L'action culturelle de la France dans le monde. Analyse critique', doctoral thesis, University of Paris I, Panthéon-Sorbonne, 1981. See also abridged version: Albert Salon, *L'action culturelle de la France dans le monde* (Paris: Nathan, 1983).

[6] Roche and Pigniau, *Histoires*.

## 1870 to 1914: Cultural Competition and Rivalries

This period is marked by the great pressure applied by political events on the running of the cultural networks of France. Britain, France, Germany, Italy, Russia and the United States were competing in the same areas and aimed to maintain or enhance their influence on the elites of other nations and they kept a watch over each other through their diplomatic and consular staffs.

Thus, in Egypt, when British influence was feared, French classes were set up staffed with teachers paid from special funds of the Foreign Affairs Ministry. The Law School of Cairo was founded in 1890, heralding the francophone higher education network.

This was also a time when French diplomats advanced and defended the use of the French language in international organizations. Roche and Pigniau cite the following example. In 1902, Jules Cambon, ambassador to Washington, realized that in the conflict between the United States and Mexico the Americans were trying to impose English as the working language at the International Court of Arbitration at The Hague. Vigorous diplomatic action, led by Delcassé, then Minister of Foreign Affairs, convinced the Danish president of the court to recognize French as 'the universal language of law and diplomacy'.[7] That situation prevailed until the Treaty of Versailles in 1919, when American President Woodrow Wilson insisted on its being expressed in both English and French.

A landmark event was the birth of the *Alliance française* in 1883, created on the initiative of French dignitaries who wished to assemble 'friends of France' in foreign parts. In many countries, local committees were established: they were organizations incorporated locally and linked to the *Alliance française* in Paris. In 1890, for example, the *Alliance française* of Melbourne was formed by French and Australian individuals. The *Alliance française* was to develop throughout the twentieth century.

In 1902, the *Mission Laïque Française* was established and it opened a number of schools before the First World War: in Salonica in 1905, Ethiopia in 1908, and Lebanon and Egypt in 1909.

In 1905, the separation of Church and state could have led to a withdrawal of aid to religious congregations in favour of direct state

---

[7] Ibid., p. 22.

control. This did not happen, and both Catholic and Protestant congregations continued to receive state aid.

During this period, the French Foreign Office concentrated on private initiatives of benefit to associations, education, health, archaeology and technology. There were several sources of funding: aid to the *Oeuvres*[8] proper, as well as covert funds; another was the *Pari Mutuel*, a state betting organization similar to the Tote: in 1909, for example, 1.5 million francs was taken from this budget to build the *Institut français* in Madrid. Some funding was also provided by the Colonial Office.

For all this time, the East was the priority of French cultural diplomacy, but that for Europe and Morocco grew steadily also. At the same time, Latin America, with the *Alliance française*, became an area for cooperation and exchanges.

In order to coordinate the lecturers sent to work abroad, the Ministry of Foreign Affairs joined with the Ministry of Public Instruction to create in 1910 the *Office national des universités et des écoles françaises*. Institutes were established in Athens, Florence, London, Madrid and St Petersburg, and higher education courses commenced in China, Egypt and Lebanon, with archaeological schools in Cairo (1880) and the Far East (1898).

## 1914 to 1920: The First World War and its Consequences

War meant these networks of association had to be realigned with regard to their usefulness in psychological warfare, the control of information and to encourage propaganda. It was at this time that proactive state habits were formed, establishing a tradition which marked out French cultural initiatives throughout the twentieth century.

In 1918, the *Service de décentralisation artistique* was created, headed by Alfred Corrot, a famous pianist, conductor and professor of music who had founded the *École normale de musique*. This service comprised two sections: international arts information and arts activities; by 1923 it had in excess of 250 correspondents abroad. In 1920, the *Service des œuvres* was reorganized into three divisions: higher education, arts activities, and

---

[8] The *Service des œuvres françaises à l'étranger* (Sofe), created in 1920, replaced the *Bureau des écoles et œuvres françaises à l'étranger*. In 1945, it was replaced by the *Direction générale des relations culturelles et des œuvres françaises à l'étranger*.

the organizations proper. The auditor of the budget at the *Chambre des députés* justified this expense in 1920 thus:

> Our Letters, our arts, our industrial civilization, our ideas, have at all times held a strong attraction for foreign nations. Our universities, our schools abroad are truly centres of propaganda in favour of France. They are a weapon in the hands of our public powers. This is why the Ministry of Foreign Affairs and its agents abroad must direct and control the initiatives, inspire and promote at all costs French intellectual penetration, with the conviction that it is one of the most efficient forms of action abroad.

## 1920 to 1939: A Dynamic Foreign Cultural Drive

The budget of the *Oeuvres* kept increasing throughout the interwar period. Between 1929 and 1938, the cultural, linguistic and humanitarian share within the Ministry of Foreign Affairs rose from 16.1 per cent to 20.4 per cent. This was a considerable increase from 1880, when the Ministry devoted only 1.9 per cent of its budget to these activities. Roche and Pigniau observe:

> The geographic earmarking of funds varies considerably between 1919 and 1939. In the East, the priority is Syria and Lebanon. The share of Europe, rather small before World War I, grows to about one third of the overall allocation. No doubt the dismemberment of the Austro-Hungarian Empire opened a new field of action in central Europe. The rise of totalitarian ideologies had led the British to create the British Council (1934). France too developed its network of European institutes: Barcelona and Naples in 1919, Zagreb in 1924, Amsterdam in 1933, Lisbon and Stockholm in 1937. Other isolated initiatives ended in establishments outside Europe: Kyoto – Paul Claudel was then ambassador in Japan – and Santiago, Chile (1938).[9]

Numerous cultural agreements – with Iran (1929), Denmark (1930), Austria and Sweden (1936) as well as Romania (1939) – offered a legal framework to the teaching of French and increasing numbers of personnel were detached from the *Instruction publique* ministry to teach French

---

[9] Roche and Pigniau, *Histoires*, p. 44.

abroad (120 in the Institutes, 130 in primary and secondary schools, 300 in universities between the two wars).


## 1939 to 1945: The Turmoil of the Second World War

During the Second World War, the stakes were not just diplomatic and military. Together with the *Alliances françaises*, the Free French gave special attention to the winning over of schools abroad and the *Alliance français* head office was transferred from Paris to London.

General de Gaulle would make clear his concept of cultural relations in a key speech made in Algiers in 1943:

> France has been able, through the centuries and up to the present drama, to maintain abroad the presence of her genius. [...] In the artistic, scientific, philosophical order, international emulation certainly is a strength mankind must not be deprived of, but higher values would not subsist without an outright psychology of intellectual nationalism. We have, once and for all, come to the conclusion that it is through free intellectual and moral relations, established between us and others, that our cultural influence can spread for the good of all, and that conversely what we are worth can grow.[10]

As the isolation of Vichy intensified, many Institutes simply closed down in Europe. Some larger Institutes and the *Alliance française* cut their links to the Vichy regime and offered their services to Free France. The *Service des œuvres*, once installed in London continued an international cultural drive, particularly in Latin America. In 1945, the *Direction générale des relations culturelles et des œuvres à l'étranger* was established to promote French cultural, scientific and technical initiatives abroad.


## 1945 to 1995: The Rise of Cultural Diplomacy and the Founding of the *Direction générale de la mondialisation*

From 1945 onwards, French foreign cultural promotion was assigned three objectives: to restore the flow of intellectual exchanges interrupted for five

---

[10] Charles De Gaulle, *Discours et messages*, vol. 1 (Paris: Club français des bibliophiles, 1971).

years; to meet the needs of those countries requiring teachers, conferences and books; and to prove the vitality of French thought despite all the recent ordeals. The overriding concern was to redefine and put back in place a policy for teaching French abroad.

This period saw the creation of the first positions of Cultural Adviser in the Embassies: some fourteen being filled in 1949. It also heralded the signing of many cultural conventions and the creation of joint commissions in charge of defining the objectives and programmes of bilateral cultural cooperation: sixty bilateral treaties were thus signed between 1945 and 1961.

French primary schools and *lycées* abroad were urged to intensify their activities, and the *Alliances françaises* also developed their teaching roles. At the same time, decolonization would bring about a redefinition of cultural activities and spawn technical cooperation aimed at helping the new authorities.

This new deal had four major goals at the end of the 1950s: to consolidate the positions of both French culture and the French language in the countries amenable to French influence, and to defend them elsewhere; to develop technical cooperation over a wider geographical context in an era of newly independent states; to maintain and strengthen traditional cultural relations, whether teaching or cultural exchanges; and to transform and integrate the cultural services of the former protectorates and the three states of Indo-China (Cambodia, Laos and Vietnam).

The 1960s saw an intensifying of cultural activities, technical cooperation, and commercial and industrial initiatives.[11] Thus, from 1961, a major training programme for the leaders of state and industry was set up in the developing countries, either by giving study grants in France or by sending experts and technicians abroad. Two distinct forms of intervention were then possible: French teaching personnel posted to Indo-China or North Africa (Morocco, Tunisia) and the local training of teachers in those countries.

Other than teaching, technical cooperation also included public administration in areas such as health, customs, postal services and finance, and technical management in industry, including electricity, agriculture and telecommunications. This form of technical cooperation

---

[11] See G. Bossuat, 'French Development Aid and Co-operation under de Gaulle', *Contemporary European History*, 12.4 (2003), pp. 431–56.

had close links with the linguistic element: cooperation was conducted in the French language.

This was a time of expansion in the cultural and technical programmes. By the end of the 1960s, there were 80 advisers and attachés, 59 Institutes and 150 cultural centres, and close to 180 French primary and secondary schools. The *Alliance française* had grown too, with over 800 committees in almost 85 countries. Over 100 film libraries were created and almost 225,000 foreign teachers were to receive help in their training to teach French.

During the 1970s, there was a broadening in scope when cultural activities were extended to the sciences. In 1979, the *Direction générale des relations culturelles, scientifiques et techniques* (DGRCST) combined the promotion of French culture and language with the scientific and technological relationships with foreign countries.

Modernization of the French foreign cultural services was organized around three key words: professionalization, exchange, and media.

*Professionalization* reflected abilities: recruitment concentrated upon practitioners of cultural affairs, coming, for example, from cultural centres or national drama centres. Professionalization also implied an effort in the initial training of personnel in France, with ongoing training in the regional meetings for cultural and artistic programmes organized throughout the world. In other respects, in the domain of teaching, developing the didactics of teaching French as a foreign language professionalized its promotion.

*Exchanges* were a second aspect of modernization. In Europe, the Goethe Institutes in France and the French Institutes in Germany organized common events. The logic clearly indicated increasing dialogue between cultures. The transition was made from a one-way effort by France towards foreign countries to a more systematic search for exchanges.

*The media* were the third aspect of this modernization. In 1984, TV5, the international satellite channel in French, commenced transmissions. Bringing together French state channels with French-speaking Swiss television, Belgian television and, since 1985, a Quebec, Canada consortium (CTQC), TV5 spread progressively outside of Europe. *Radio France Internationale* rose from twenty-seventh to rank eighth in the world, and has developed considerably in recent years.

The landmark event at the end of this period was undoubtedly the profound upheaval of Europe following the fall of the Berlin Wall and the implosion of the Soviet Union between 1989 and 1991. New cultural establishments were created in Bulgaria, Estonia, Romania, Russia and

Ukraine. An audio-visual aspect accompanied numerous initiatives of scientific and technical cooperation.

This historical review ends with the major reform of 1995, directed by Alain Juppé, Minister for Foreign Affairs, and organized around four main ideas: advancing foreign relations by restructuring and bringing together the cultural and linguistic sections; decentralizing and accelerating personnel management procedures; adopting measures for both quantitative and qualitative evaluation; and offering new career paths to those involved.

An important reform, it sought to review the foreign-based missions, their organization and funding in the execution of French foreign cultural policies. It initiated the thinking expressed in numerous reports and ministerial decrees between 1996 and 2010, which are examined in the next chapter, and are a sign of the reflections leading to an overhaul of the French diplomatic service, with the spread of globalization and changing strategies of influence.

The creation of the *Direction générale de la mondialisation, du développement et des partenariats* is without doubt the most important reform since the merging of the Ministry of Foreign Affairs with that for Cooperation in 1998. This is a global project to engage the cultural and scientific networks with world debates on matters such as economic and financial regulation, climate, health, education and sustainable growth. This department is a merger of the *Direction générale de la coopération international et du développement*, the *Direction des affaires économiques et financiers* and the *Sous-direction des affaires économiques de la Direction des Nations unies et des organisations internationales*. The global economy and development strategies, state global wealth, cultural and linguistic policies, policies of mobility and attractiveness are some of the new department's responsibilities.

Thus, the cultural and scientific elements are now essential to the foreign activities of France. They are also one aspect of a wider plan integrating economic and societal issues. This is what Marie-Christine Kessler aptly demonstrates when she writes:

> For so many years the Foreign Affairs ministry has developed a policy deliberately associating culture and economy as a part of regular bilateral events in France as well as abroad. The idea is twofold: on the one hand these events are in part funded by companies the partnership of which is sought on such occasions; on the other hand, they are offered a new or improved base in the target countries with the official backing of

France, thus conferring on their presence an exceptional springboard and publicity.[12]

The economic dimension of culture is thus given its full meaning within the framework of international cooperation.[13]

Nowadays, cultural and scientific diplomacy is recognized as an important element of influence and cooperation, as was evident from a Ditchley Foundation (UK) seminar in 2012:

> There were comparatively few specific, practical recommendations. The sense was more that we were in the middle of a paradigm shift where everything would need to change in one way or another, and all the old models needed to be re-examined. But there were a few fundamental areas where new efforts were urgently needed:
>
> • above all, devising and agreeing a new rationale for cultural diplomacy which could convince governments and others that it was not only still worth supporting, but needed new resources, without at the same time increasing government control over what was being done;
>
> • along with this, a new attempt to find ways of defining and expressing its impact, without falling into the trap of looking for simple numbers which purported to do this;
>
> • more research was needed on what worked and what didn't, and on comparative models of action and funding, building on what existed already;
>
> • new ways of engaging and involving the corporate world were also needed, with public–private partnerships the preferred model;
>
> • the possibility of joint international efforts at cultural diplomacy should be explored more thoroughly, where individual national promotion was not the point, but the conveying of ideas and values to a particular audience or region.[14]

[12] Marie-Christine Kessler, 'L'apport de la culture à la diplomatie économique', *Géoéconomie*, 56 (winter 2010–11), pp. 1–15.

[13] Françoise Benhamou, *Les dérèglements de l'exception culturelle: plaidoyer pour une perspective européenne* (Paris: Le Seuil, 2006).

[14] The Ditchley Foundation, 'Cultural Diplomacy: Does it Work?' <www.ditchley.co.uk/conferences/past-programme/2010-2019/2012/cultural-diplomacy> Accessed 9 November 2012.

## 2

# Cultural and Scientific Action since 1995: Soft Power or Hard Power?

### A New Paradigm?

Cultural and scientific diplomacy is currently topical. When Barack Obama was elected President of the United States in 2008, initial comments, followed by the primary political decisions (notably in the domain of scientific diplomacy) presaged the return of what is termed *soft power*, a peaceful means of influence, as opposed to *hard power*, a more coercive approach which can include use of military force.[1] It was during 2008 and 2009 that the expression 'diplomacy of influence' appeared in France to characterize the country's cultural and scientific efforts abroad. This was what was required of Japan in its 1947 constitution, which obliged the country to give up armed intervention after the Second World War. Japan then embarked upon a significant programme to develop *soft power* – the 'Japan cool' – notably through comic strips, cartoons and other film and television successes.[2]

From the French perspective, the question is whether the country is going to lose the battle of *soft power*? In his article, 'Culture: pourquoi la France va perdre la bataille du "Soft Power"', Frédéric Martel writes:

The cartography of cultural exchanges undergoes transformations. We witness a rise in power of global mainstream entertainment, mostly

[1] Joseph S. Nye, *Bound to Lead: The Changing Nature of American Power* (New York: Basic Books, 1990); Paul M. Kennedy, *The Rise and Fall of the Great Powers: Economic Change and Military conflict from 1500 to 2000* (New York: Random House, 1987); Xavier Greffe and Sylvie Pflieger, *La politique culturelle en France* (Paris: La Documentation française, 2009).

[2] See Greffe and Pflieger, *La politique culturelle en France*, p. 202.

American, and the emergence of regional blocs. Furthermore, national cultures are everywhere strengthened, despite the 'other' reference, the 'other' culture being that of the United States. Last, there is an accelerating tendency to fuse influences: American entertainment is often produced by European, Japanese or, increasingly, Indian multinationals and at the same time local cultures are frequently produced by Hollywood. [...] In this new landscape, Europe finds it very hard to find its place, and France is losing the battle of *soft power*.[3]

Martel's diagnosis is harsh and certainly needs qualification. Nevertheless, according to this former cultural attaché to the United States, it still has several operational consequences.

The separation of the cultural from the diplomatic is seen as crucial in order to establish the independence of the cultural network. It is vital to assert the autonomy of research and to detach the debate of ideas from the diplomatic service as we enter the digital age. Art must be separated from the embassies, to allow professionals to concentrate on negotiating with the cable operators, with Internet access providers, television production companies, mobile telephone operators and media groups, instead of organizing art film showings and cultural suppers for ambassadors.

Faced with these criticisms, four proposals and priorities have been mooted. The first would be to create agencies for the media, creative and cultural industries in the main capitals, headed by professionals with recognized expertise in at least one of these domains, trained and appointed for a longer period than is presently the case. The second proposal made by Martel is to create a centre attached to the French president's office, modelled after the *Centre d'analyse économique*, for the analysis of and to forecast needs. Headed by specialists in international affairs, these centres could provide researchers with time-limited projects with a remit to produce tangible results. The third recommendation would be to overhaul the *Direction générale de la mondialisation, du développement et des partenariats* of the European and Foreign Affairs Ministry in order to cover culture, digital issues, soft power, development, negotiations for television rights for sport and the influence of talk shows. Last, France should be equipped with an effective Internet portal for

---

[3] Frédéric Martel, 'Culture: pourquoi la France va perdre la bataille du "Soft Power"', Terra Nova – Note 1/10 (31 March 2010), p. 2 <www.tnova.fr/sites/default/files/252-martel.pdf>.

culture and the debate of ideas, which could be attached to the new agency.

Whether or not this is a revolution worthy of Copernicus, the diagnosis makes no concessions, and the proposals are radical. So we must put these investigations, polemic at times, back in the context of the numerous reports and questions which have been punctuating French reflections on cultural and scientific diplomacy for a decade. This should allow the identifying of strengths and weaknesses in the country's cultural and scientific organization abroad and show the necessary relationship between the agencies created in July 2010 and the diplomatic and consular network of France.

The challenges for this new cultural and scientific diplomacy are considerable. There is an imperative to strengthen cultural and scientific initiatives in the face of the continuing globalization of culture. This issue is at the heart of a report from the Jean Jaurès Foundation in 2012:

> What place has culture, a term which in French can be interpreted equally as a process as well as an output, in French foreign policy? It can be a sphere of action as much as an additional lever of influence for a given policy or it can be an autonomous policy in its own right with its own objectives. In this latter case, a distinction must be made between means and ends. While France still has a number of assets as a significant world cultural power, it seems to have lost its ability to conceptualize ways of using this power effectively.[4]

This being the case, it would be useful to align the map of cultural and scientific networks with the new world order in the following ways:

- to strengthen the cultural networks in developing countries through art, culture and heritage sites;

- to make local appointments where there are insufficient existing resources to ensure results; and

- to improve and adapt links with other French cultural bodies, such as the *Alliance française.*

---

[4] Jean Jaurès Foundation, 'L'action culturelle extérieure de la France', Les GRECs, groupes d'études et de recherches sur la culture, Note 143 (19 July 2012) <www.jean-jaures. org/Publications/Les-notes/L-action-culturelle-exterieure-de-la-France/(language)/ fre-FR>.

The Jean Jaurès Foundation report also emphasizes the need for an inter-ministerial policy to extend France's cultural and scientific influence through closer association with the work of the Ministry of Foreign Affairs, French cultural networks abroad, the Culture Ministry, Education and Higher Education Ministries, and the principal national cultural and scientific bodies:

- to establish an inter-ministerial council for state action abroad;

- to set up an online resource with relevant information about the networks;

- to encourage staff to rotate between different institutions; and

- to improve the dialogue between scientific and technical foreign aid with cultural and linguistic policies.

Reforms carried out in 2010 allow for a new framework for foreign aid. It is vital to see how effective this will be in helping the diplomatic missions and other bodies.

## Three New Agencies for 2010

A law of 27 July 2010 relating to foreign affairs of state established three public bodies charged with the foreign activities of France that will have the task of promoting the country's presence and influence abroad and participating in foreign affairs of the state, in particular by implementing cultural activities, cooperation and partnerships abroad.[5] These public establishments are under the supervision of the state, which specifies their mission statements and the determines the logistics of their functioning and organization. A long-term convention between the French state and each public establishment contributing to France's foreign policies defines the objectives and the means necessary to fulfilling these requirements.

This law provided for a new public body for industry and commerce – *Établissement public à caractère industriel et commercial* (*Epic*) – to be known as *CampusFrance*. *CampusFrance* replaces the *Egide* association,

    [5] Loi no 2010-873 du 27 juillet 2010 relative à l'action extérieure de l'Etat <www.legifrance.gouv.fr/affichTexte.do?cidTexte=JORFTEXT000022521532>.

the prime agency for international exchange facilities in France, and the former existing public interest group, also known as *CampusFrance*.

The new agency is responsible for developing and promoting abroad French higher education and professional training opportunities, receiving foreign students and researchers, managing grants, trainee programmes and other international exchanges for students and researchers, and promoting and developing higher education particularly by electronic means.

The new agency *CampusFrance* operates to directions defined jointly by the European and Foreign Affairs Ministry, the Ministry of Higher Education and Research and the Ministry of Immigration, Integration, National Identity and Fair Development.

To fulfil its responsibilities, this state body was charged with liaising with the diplomatic network abroad, under the authority of the diplomatic mission heads together with establishments under their authority or tied by convention to the embassies and consulates.

One last step, scheduled for the end of 2011: all the international activities of the *Centre national des œuvres universitaires et scolaires (Cnous)* to be integrated into the new agency *CampusFrance*, the process to be described in a report submitted to the French government in the June of that year.

The law of 27 July 2010 also provides for the creation of another industrial and commercial public establishment, the *Institut français*, placed under the remit of the European and Foreign Affairs Ministry. This contributes abroad to cultural and linguistic diversity in a spirit of partnership with the host countries. The *Institut français*, with the help of the French cultural network abroad, provides an input to the foreign cultural policy defined by the European and Foreign Affairs Ministry, in concert with the ministry in charge of culture. Its duties include:

- a presence abroad for and the promotion of French culture;

- the development of exchanges with other European cultures, including those of francophone Europe;

- support for the creation, development and spread of artistic expression in the less-developed South, as well reciprocal promotion and diffusion in France and elsewhere;

- the distribution of film and television heritage, in dialogue with the organizations active in these fields;

- the promotion and dissemination abroad of French ideas, culture and knowledge;

- support for the widest possible circulation of publications, works and authors;

- the promotion, dissemination and teaching abroad of the French language;

- training for members of the French cultural network abroad, for foreign institutions and professionals within the French cultural offer; and

- counselling and professional training of French and foreign personnel contributing to these activities. As such, the *Institut français* is associated with the recruiting, posting and career management policy of these key personnel.

In a way similar to that of *CampusFrance*, the *Institut français* calls upon the diplomatic network abroad, under the authority of the diplomatic mission heads, and the establishments under the authority of, or tied by convention to, these diplomatic missions. The *Institut français* also collaborates with European and international organizations, French regional and local authorities, professional organizations concerned with the exporting of the French cultural industries, home and foreign institutions involved in the creation and distribution of French culture, as well with the private and state partners such as the *Alliances françaises*.

Thus, the *Institut français* must contribute to the direction and management of the cultural network, taking over from the *Cultures France* association. From 1 January 2011, the new *Institut français* was set other remits such as the cinema, the debate of ideas, the coordination of cultural seasons and 'joint years' such as that of France–Russia in 2010, together with the training and management of personnel.

The third agency created was *France Expertise Internationale*. Also placed under the aegis of the European and Foreign Affairs Ministry, it contributes to the promotion of French technical assistance and international expertise abroad, as well as the supervision of projects with bilateral or multilateral funding. This agency also addresses the needs of the diplomatic network abroad and replaced the former *France coopération internationale.*

These three agencies thus play an essential part in the cultural and scientific roles of France, in close collaboration with the diplomatic and consular corps.

## A Sweeping Reform

In his letter of 28 October 2009 to all members of the cultural and scientific networks, Bernard Kouchner, then Minister of European and Foreign Affairs, justified the necessary reform of France's foreign cultural policy in these words:

> The erosion of budgetary means, the absence of a clear and long-term strategy, the unsatisfactory management of the career paths of agents as well as a lack of specific training, the poor visibility of our organization, in Paris and abroad, have led to a discouraging of those in our foreign cultural service and to increased criticism.

He announced a significant reform to French foreign cultural policy. This reform established the foundations of a strategy of influence for France. This is based on a better organized ministry to pilot foreign cultural activities – a 'ministry of globalization' to address the world issues of the day and to activate the necessary diplomacy of influence. Seen as a reinforcement, it would be the role of not one but three agencies in charge of promoting ideas, language, culture and knowledge. A unified local network would be formed by the coming together of the cultural services in the embassies and financially autonomous bodies.

Additional funds were planned to boost foreign cultural affairs, this reform receiving an exceptional endowment of €40 million in 2009 and 2010.

This reorganization of the Ministry of European and Foreign Affairs and of its foreign cultural services was made in several stages. After the publication on 11 July 2008 of a White Paper on European and foreign policy, the *Livre blanc sur la politique étrangère et européenne de la France,*[6]

---

[6] 'La France et l'Europe dans le monde' <www.diplomatie.gouv.fr/fr/IMG/pdf/2LIVREBLANC_DEF.pdf>.

came the creation on 16 March 2009 of the *Direction générale de la mondialisation, du développement et des partenariats*; on 10 July 2009, conclusion of the work of the exploratory mission headed by the general secretary; and then, on 22 July, came the passage by the Council of Ministers of a bill concerning the foreign activities of the state, which provided for the creation of two industrial and commercial state bodies – one for international expertise and exchanges, the other for French cultural activities abroad.[7] The actual law would propose forming two establishments instead of one. Before arriving at this final version of July 2010, a major audit of the agents of the cultural and scientific networks was carried out on the content and introduction of a training plan, as well as the future nature and logistics of relations between the networks and future state establishments.

In fact, the Ministry of European and Foreign Affairs does not have a responsibility to assume control of all of the foreign cultural policies but rather to define priorities and strategies, to oversee the links between cultural initiatives and foreign policy and to facilitate the realization of the cultural projects abroad. It is thus necessary to improve the present organization to serve creative artists, professionals of culture, scientists and researchers of influence. This presupposes defining both a coherent general plan with efficient and appropriate strategies by sector, as well as adapting the administrative tools and human interfaces in order to obtain best value for the state.

This would entail the necessity of a global policy for a cultural presence, supported by clear operational strategies by sector for each geographical location. The streamlining of the network abroad was seen as important, particularly following the merging of the services of cooperation and cultural activities with the centres under the denomination of *Instituts français*, which were given financial autonomy. The management of each *Insitut français* would represent a cultural agency locally. The new agency would have the responsibility for training policies for personnel.

---

[7] This consultation process was entrusted to Delphine Borione, Director of Cultural Policy and the French Language at the European and Foreign Affairs Ministry.

## The French Cultural Network: A Subject of National Debate

French foreign cultural policy is currently the subject of some debate. Bernard de Montferrand, French Ambassador in Germany, commented:

> In most cases, we do not do everything ourselves; we do 'cultural engineering' and our local partners act on our behalf. The cost of the French cultural network abroad is equivalent to that of the annual subsidy to the Paris Opera.[8]

This network also provides many jobs in France. It is thus important to underline the necessary relationship between the embassies and institutions of the cultural network, in Paris as well as in foreign parts. The activities of a cultural institute cannot be separated from that of an embassy. According to De Montferrand, 'The cultural dialogue embraces all the major debates in society which are the daily fare of embassies'.[9] There is a need to develop the network of *Instituts français* and to have the support of a cultural agency capable of mobilizing French creative artists in the service of this network of influence around the world. This question divides partisans of a separation between powers and institutions from the proponents of necessary cooperation between all concerned.[10] Should cultural institutions be given more independence from political and diplomatic bodies? How is France to promote the development of European and multilateral cultural policies?

The approach taken in this volume is to emphasize the necessarily complementary nature of the national cultural and scientific institutions to the diplomatic and consular network with the attached cultural, scientific and technical organizations. This is what we can deduce from the many reports on the subject during the last decade or so.[11]

---

[8] Bernard de Montferrand, 'Il ne faut pas tuer le réseau culturel français' [We must not kill the French cultural network], *Libération* (9 April 2010).

[9] Ibid.

[10] See Volker Steinkamp, 'Die Auswärtige Kulturpolitik als Instrument der französischen Außenpolitik' [Foreign cultural policy as an instrument of the foreign policy of France], Deutsche Gesellschaft für Auswärtige Politik, DGAP-Analyse, 5 (August 2009).

[11] References in Julia Kristeva-Joyaux, 'Le message culturel de la France et la vocation interculturelle de la francophonie'. Avis du Conseil économique, social et environnemental présenté par Julia Kristeva-Joyaux, rappporteur, au nom de la section des relations extérieures (Paris: CESE, 2009).

The report by Julia Kristeva-Joyaux aspires 'to give our cultural message a second wind which will enable it to implement, with audacity and creativity, a dynamic multicultural policy open on the world'.[12] Kristeva-Joyaux asserts that every parliamentary report in the last ten years has underlined this necessity, without this having a real impact on the political measures taken. Yet the necessity of such a reflection is all the more urgent since globalization makes imperative the establishing of a cultural and scientific policy that can adapt to the pressures of the day. The measures advocated are diverse. To achieve diversity, promotion of French culture abroad must be made more coherent, more inter-ministerial. What is needed is the rationalization and renewal of a cultural network that for the last few years has been looking increasingly like a simple stacking up of initiatives, such as cooperation and cultural activities services, scientific services, *Instituts français*, *Alliances françaises* and the French state-run primary and secondary schools. There is a need in Western Europe and in the industrialized countries for cooperation between institutions and for a strengthening of the network in the emerging countries.

The reform which passed into law was the culmination of parliamentary work over a decade which entailed numerous reports. The first, in 2001, was by Yves Dauge, a member of the *Assemblée nationale*.[13] In the cultural domain, the important feature was the merging of the cultural networks abroad (comprising 140 establishments) with the corresponding *Instituts français*. Around ten diplomatic missions form a representative sample of the diverse diplomatic posts and would lead to a three-year experiment, producing each year an evaluation report for the French parliament. At the request of the senate, a strategic council of orientation would be created to enable close oversight of all the partners in the French cultural and scientific diplomatic community.

Cooperation between the Ministries of European and Foreign Affairs, of Culture and Communication, and of Higher Education and Research was essential. This contrasts with the situation in the United Kingdom, where cultural activities enjoy greater autonomy. French cultural and scientific diplomacy dictates close collaboration between the relevant

---

[12] Ibid., p. 128.

[13] Assemblée nationale, Rapport déposé en application de l'article 145 du règlement par la Commission des affaires étrangères sur les centres culturels français à l'étranger et présenté par M. Yves Dauge, député (February 2001).

ministries: Higher Education and Research for *Campus France*, Culture and Communication for the *Institut français*. For French cultural influence abroad, the Ministry for Culture and Communication has traditionally acted at different levels. The first step is the staging of foreign cultural events in France and the reception and training of foreign professionals of culture from abroad by means of support given to festivals and cultural events (primarily the object is the reception of foreign cultures, as well as the organization of cultural seasons). The offer of expertise is made, particularly with regard to cultural heritage. Cooperation is fostered in the cinematographic industry, led by the *Centre national du cinéma et de l'image animée* (CNC – formerly the *Centre national de la cinématographie*). Literary cooperation comes under the leadership of the *Centre national du livre* (CNL), the *Bureau international de l'édition française* and the *Centrale de l'édition*.

This new coordinated approach implied a budgetary regrouping of the finance assigned to French international initiatives, a realignment of the geographic priorities of the various bodies, coordination of the international efforts of state establishments, as well as inter-ministerial dialogue of the political nature of influence. These governmental priorities go hand in hand with the organization of cultural and scientific posts, which in turn demands a dialogue and teamwork vital to such a policy of cooperation. This is all the more true because the key word, when one undertakes cooperation within any country, is *partnership*: this must apply just as much to the multiple services leading the interests of France as to the services of the country where the activities take place.

## Cultural and Scientific Diplomacy: An International Issue

Cultural diplomacy, in its broadest sense, has become an international issue. Rod Fisher identifies the seven main objectives of an international cultural policy. These are:

- to promote cultural diplomacy;

- to develop cultural relations;

- to support the export of cultural goods and products of the creative industries;

- to favour the development of new partnership arrangements;

- to attract tourism and investment;

- to improve the programmes aimed at helping the developing nations of the South; and

- to generate a positive, informed and favourable image of the instigating country.[14]

Increasingly, cultural diplomacy is developing in two new and complementary directions: the arrival of new actors on the one hand and the development of a multilateral approach on the other. In fact, as Steve Green notes, the most important change in recent years is the evolution towards a multipolar world, with the growing influence of Asia in general and China in particular.[15] The development of the Confucius Institutes is indeed spectacular. Since they were created in 2004, more than 300 have been opened in over eighty countries. The objective is to achieve 1,000 centres around the world. That is as many as are represented in the present network of *Alliances françaises*. Each Confucius Institute is formed in a host university with the help of a corresponding Chinese university and offers a programme of activities centred upon language and arts. In addition, they organize increasing numbers of seminars on the recent history of China and current policies.

If China is undoubtedly the most active country internationally, it is also true that Korea intends to develop its cultural network – from thirty-five centres in 2010 to 150 by 2015. The same is true for India, Indonesia, Vietnam, Malaysia and other Asian countries presently reviewing their cultural diplomacy.

What is true in the cultural domain also applies in the scientific. The OECD is developing new science and technology programmes to address

[14]   Rod Fisher, 'Recognising the Significance of Culture in Government and EU External Relations', in *Mobility Matters: Programmes and Schemes to Support the Mobility of Artists and Cultural Professionals. Final Report*. An ERICarts Institute Study for the European Commission (DG Education and Culture) (October 2008) <http://ec.europa.eu/culture/key-documents/doc/ericarts/final_report_ERICarts.pdf>.

[15]   Steve Green (Team Leader for the European Union National Institutes for Culture (Eunic) Presidency), 'New Directions', 'La acción cultural exterior en perspectiva estratégica: tendencias de futuro', conference, Instituto Cervantes et Real Instituto Elcano, Madrid, 14–15 December 2009.

the latest global challenges.[16] Areas of concern are notably climate change, food security, energy and infectious diseases.

We finish this survey by mentioning a recent United States diplomatic report, 'Public Diplomacy; Strengthening US Engagement with the World: A Strategic Approach for the 21st Century',[17] which relates traditional cultural and scientific diplomacy to the new global issues of the day: democracy and human rights, the fight against violent extremism, nuclear non-proliferation and economic prosperity, in addition to the global themes stated above.

---

[16] Organization for Economic Cooperation and Development (OECD), 'New Approaches and Governance Mechanisms for Multilateral Cooperation in Science, Technology and Innovation to Address Global Challenges', Project Rationale and Relevance (17 March 2010).

[17] Office of the Under Secretary of State for Public Diplomacy and Public Affairs, 'Public Diplomacy; Strengthening US Engagement with the World: A Strategic Approach for the 21st Century' (26 February 2010).

# 3

# The Protagonists of Cultural
# and Scientific Diplomacy;
# 2011: A New Start

In the autumn of 2010, two new initiatives were significant. First, a more coherent and comprehensive organization came into being. This new agency, *Cultures France*,[1] was to rely on the support of the 145 Cultural Institutes and Centres abroad, gaining enhanced functions due to their merging with the cultural services of the embassies, which would be its foothold and use the same name – *Insitut français*. French cultural diplomacy would thus advance in the world under one name, one brand – essential in an age of globalization. The agency, in Paris and at centres around the world, was to maintain a permanent working relationship in the programming of activities and the management of personnel and finance. In around ten of the diplomatic posts, a formal legal attachment of the network to the agency was to be trialled until 2013, in each case obliging the formation of an integrated organization.

The nascent agency was to take on the functions of the *CulturesFrance* association, which it was to replace. It would thus promote artists and cultural content, such as books, the theatre, cinema and the visual arts. It would also develop new missions, the most fundamental being the promotion of the French language. It would aid the spread of the ideas, knowledge and scientific culture of the country and ensure France a presence in the great debates that stir the world. Training the personnel who contribute to the foreign cultural policy of France would be a further function.

The *Institut français* was to be a state industrial and commercial

---

[1] 'En 2011 Culturesfrance devient INSTITUT FRANÇAIS' <http://web.archive.org/web/20101223173840/http://www.culturesfrance.com/culturesfrance-presentation.html>.

undertaking, a status that offers more flexible management and allows evolution in a competitive context. This status would also allow it to anchor the organization in the public domain.

The agency would associate more comprehensively all those who contribute to French foreign cultural policy, in particular the Ministry of Culture and Communication, the large cultural establishments, French regional and local authorities and representatives of the cultural, audiovisual and digital culture industries. All were to have a place in the governance of the agency, to guarantee legitimacy. A new partnership would be established with the *Alliances françaises*, which complemented and extended that of the *Institut français*.

## The Role of the Ministry of Culture and Communication

Dialogue between the Ministry of European and Foreign Affairs and the Ministry of Culture and Communication is vital: such dialogue created the *Institut français* agency, and it demanded an ongoing common definition of strategy, as the law of 27 July 2010 expressly states. Close synergies between the two ministries were to be exploited in order to keep French cultural initiatives constantly under review and better to serve and promote French culture and heritage abroad. In cinema and the cultural industries, for example, facilitating the movement of works of art or of authors can only be achieved through close collaboration between the Ministry of Culture and Communication, the *Centre national du cinéma et de l'image animée* (CNC) and the *Centre national du livre* (CNL), together with the organizations charged with the export of culture: *Unifrance* for the promotion of French cinema around the world since 1949 and, under the aegis of the CNC, the *Bureau export de la musique française*, and, for book publishing, the *Bureau international de l'édition française*.

The promotion of live performances and fine arts was also to be undertaken by the *Institut français*. For artists as well as for the French cultural institutions, the circulation of their works internationally is of economic importance as well for their reputation. An essential tool for this promotion would be the development of a network of artists' residencies in France, and, reciprocally, would better employ exchange facilities abroad to welcome artists from France. Improved coordination and information are much needed, and such tasks are well suited to this institute.

In a multicultural, globalized age, the demand for prominence is a fundamental challenge for cultural diplomacy. For this very reason, the *Institut français* must play an essential role regarding information on what French culture can offer, particularly on the Internet. This permanent exhibition on the Web is a priority – one this author would like to see extended by the digitizing of the national heritage collection. It is *par excellence* a domain where the activities undertaken by the *Institut français*, the French Foreign Office and the Ministry for Culture and Communication can be considered in a global context, so as to offer to the general public abroad and to specialists in partner countries as wide as possible access to reference information. The better informed the world is of what is on offer culturally from France, the more readily they can welcome such to their theatres and other cultural establishments.

Amongst the new assignments assigned to the *Institut français*, the training of personnel for the cultural network abroad was also to be a breakthrough. The objective is systematically to offer each cultural diplomat complete training in the cultural professions. From 2010, cooperation between the two ministries has intensified, so as to increase the number of candidates for training.

One of the great challenges for a French international presence is also the dissemination of the French language abroad. Logically it is for the Ministry of Culture and Communication to drive and coordinate French linguistic policy, but the fact that the *Institut français* undertakes this essential foreign role should lead to new ways of promoting the French language, particularly via the Internet.

It is quite clear that, for each of its responsibilities, the *Institut français* needs to call upon the experience and expertise of the Ministry for Culture and Communication and its sphere of influence, given that international efforts have assumed a fundamental importance. Within this ministry, its great museums, the national stage, its establishments of higher education are the breeding ground that the influence of French culture abroad cannot do without.

Thus the *Institut français* would become a transmitter of culture – not only of French culture abroad, but also reciprocally of other cultures entering France by means of cultural seasons and years of culture dedicated to various partner countries. This welcoming of foreign cultures within the French cultural space is indeed essential. A culture can live and bloom only in dialogue and exchange with creators and artists from other cultures.

## The Essential Role
## of the Ministry for Higher Education and Research

There are several objectives for international cooperation in research and innovation:

- to strengthen the scientific excellence of France by a variety of strategic alliances;

- to strengthen, similarly, the technological excellence of France and its potential for innovation;

- to consolidate the position of France as a world power in science and technology;

- to attract to the French scientific community the best players so as to enhance the excellence of French research and higher education;

- to contribute to international research initiatives to tackle global challenges; and

- to contribute to French commitments of support for developing countries.

International cooperation between researchers when it arises is advanced by their supervising organizations, which sign formal agreements with their foreign counterparts. Increasingly, establishments are implementing strategies that take the form of joint research programmes and structures with foreign research organizations and bureaux of representation. The French ministries foster this cooperation by encouraging French researchers to collaborate with foreign colleagues through a series of incentives. There is also a significant French commitment to international organizations supporting scientific research through participating in major research initiatives and funding for international programmes of fundamental research, applied to or in support of developing countries.

For research generally, higher education and research establishments, the universities and research bodies engage in international cooperation supported by their research units which can take the form of virtual laboratories, joint international laboratories or networks of excellence in research and training with a European or international dimension. The services of the state can help to strengthen cooperation deemed to be strategic value; following scientific and viability evaluations, means can be offered to laboratories to develop international cooperation as centres of excellence.

In other instances, in order to further new strategies of cooperation, the Ministry for Higher Education and Research, often in conjunction with the Ministry of European and Foreign Affairs, will call for tenders to stimulate themes for cooperation in original research. According to the Internet site of the ministry, almost 42 per cent of research finance in France is for international scientific cooperation.

### French Regional and Local Authorities and Development Aid

'Decentralized cooperation is an invaluable means of creating collective security and prosperity', stated Jean-Michel Severino, former Director General of the *Agence française de développement* (AFD),[2] and this is a major instrument of influence. French local authorities have mounted cooperation projects with the support of regional prefectures and in partnership with the Foreign Office since 2008. Decentralized cooperation is defined as the international initiatives of regional authorities, namely twinning opportunities, development projects, technical exchanges and operations of economic promotion.[3] In this area, local authorities can provide significant support by involving the main players such as network associations, professional organizations, hospitals and business. The main objectives are:

- to encourage decentralized cooperation in regional and local authorities' development by placing emphasis on the local government sector and local economic development through calls for projects;

- to provide initial support for decentralized cooperation in the partner areas (sub-Saharan Africa, the Mediterranean and the French-speaking countries);

[2] Jean-Michel Severino, 'Quel avenir pour la coopération décentralisée' (24 November 2010) <www.cncd.fr/frontoffice/article.asp?aid=554&menuid=559&lv=3>.

[3] Missions du ministère des Affaires étrangères et européennes, 'Orientations françaises pour l'action internationale des collectivités territoriales', Direction générale de la mondialisation, du développement durable et des partenariats (2010) <www.cncd.fr/frontoffice/file.asp?id=353>.

- to favour a regional approach involving several countries in an area such as the Niger basin or the Balkans;

- to integrate this decentralized cooperation into an approach to development centred on advancement;

- to strengthen the economic presence of France, involving the French centre for foreign trade and the agency *Ubifrance* (formerly the *Centre français du commerce extérieur* CFCE);[4] and

- to mobilize the cultural diversity of the French overseas territories.

Within the framework of the call for projects of 2011, three geographic partnerships have been given priority: economic development and local governance in sub-Saharan Africa, in Comoros, Haiti and Madagascar, and, most notably, local governance in the countries of the Mediterranean Union. Besides these three geographic partnerships, the call for projects includes four thematic programmes to promote cooperation with all countries eligible for official development assistance other than the emerging countries: agriculture and food; water and sanitation; sustainable tourism and the promotion of natural and cultural heritage; and the fight against the digital divide.

The developing countries are the partners of French regional and local authorities in such priority areas as local governance, economic development and self-sufficiency in agriculture. The emerging countries are invited into partnerships relating to innovation, sustainable development, measures relating to climate and cooperation in science and higher education.[5] The *Commission nationale de la coopération décentralisée* (CNCD) is the nominated instrument of dialogue between the state and the local authorities: it outlines the strategic directions for international action by these authorities. The *Délégation pour l'action extérieure des collectivités territoriales* (DAECT) for local authorities' foreign affairs works closely with the networks involved in decentralized cooperation: the *Association*

---

[4] Industrial and commercial public body under the control of the Ministre de l'Economie, de l'Industrie et de l'Emploi, of the Secrétaire chargé du Commerce extérieur, and of the Direction générale du Trésor. Its mission is to facilitate French companies in exporting goods and to advance their presence in foreign markets via its sixty-four missions in forty-four countries.

[5] The *Atlas français de la coopération décentralisée* is available at <www.diplomatie.gouv.fr/fr/enjeux-internationaux/cooperation-decentralisee/atlas-francais-de-la-cooperation>.

*des maires de France*, for the several thousand mayors, the *Association des Régions de France*, *Cités unies France*, representing the towns, and the *Association française du conseil des communes et régions de l'Europe*, for the regions and local parishes of the country.[6]

## The Multilateral Setting:
## Initiatives of the European Union and of UNESCO

*The External Cultural Strategy of the European Union*
At the meeting of the directors-general for the external cultural relations of the European Union, presided over by Belgium from 22 to 24 September 2010, several themes were addressed: the cultural dialogue between the Mediterranean countries and Europe, discussions on a timetable of work for the Council of Europe to promote culture and a proposed common platform to present the cultural organizations of the member states.

Dialogue between the European Union and the Arab countries around the theme of modernity, concerning such things as the media, the status of women and the cultural space of resistance, centred upon support for existing organizations, including the Union for the Mediterranean and the Anna Lindh Foundation. For the media, there are the initiatives of the Arab States Broadcasting Union (Asbu) and, for broadcasting, the *Conférence permanente de l'audiovisuel méditerranéen (Copeam)*. The expertise of the European Union, particularly in matters of regulation, could be useful; the training of professionals should also be supported. It is significant that the Conference on the Internet and Freedom of Speech, jointly organized with the Netherlands, due to take place in Paris in October 2010, was cancelled.

In culture, the priorities are of twofold: to foster an awareness of the European Union 2020 strategy highlighting the potential of culture in matters of creativity and innovation, notably the support of cultural enterprise; and to recognize the role of culture in the fight against poverty and social exclusion. The draft conclusion concerned continuing education, intercultural dialogue and citizenship was adopted at the 'Culture Council' of November 2010.

---

[6] Serge Tomasi (directeur de l'économie globale et des stratégies du développement), 'Document-Cadre français de coopération au développement, XVIIIe Conférence des ambassadeurs, 27 August 2010.

Beyond these two major priorities, several issues are on the agenda. These include:

- the strategic objectives of the European Agenda for Culture 2007–13, the evaluation of the action plan 2008–10 and the formulation of a new post-2010 work schedule, adopted at the November 2010 'Culture Council';

- the adoption of the European heritage label – a French initiative;

- the digitization of film theatres; and

- the awareness campaign of the European Commission on the necessity for reviewing the audiovisual production chain in its entirety: development, production and circulation.

The European Agenda for Culture 2011–14 has four priorities for action:

- cultural diversity, intercultural dialogue and an inclusive Europe;

- the cultural and creative industries;

- expertise and mobility; and

- the role of culture in external relations.

An inventory of the foreign cultural initiatives of all twenty-seven countries of the European Union is at the planning stage. This data bank, hosted by the European Commission, on the Circa platform, should make it possible to publicize the programmes each member state undertakes in any country around the world. At first, only the cultural sectors will be addressed (such as the promotion of a country's language, support for the cultural industries, broadcasting, culture and development), to be followed by cooperation through schools and higher education. This is intended to be an operational tool, simple to use and to keep up to date.

EUNIC, the European Union National Institutes for Culture network, brings together the national cultural institutions of the European Union.[7] It was established in 2006 to form an umbrella group for the cultural institutes of the various countries, and now accounts for over two million language learners, with 25,000 personnel in 150 countries.

Steve Green, director general of EUNIC, characterizes the geographic

---

[7] <www.eunic-online.eu>.

priorities as Brazil, Russia, India and China, as well as the countries bordering the European Union. This diplomacy of influence integrates the classic dissemination and promotion of culture and language, but there is now an emphasis on themes – culture and development, the creative industries – and on fostering the multilateral rather than the bilateral, together with a more individualized approach to initiatives based on mutual understanding rather than simple promotion. If the project is to be a success, the organization must be flexible, avoid excluding countries with little cultural infrastructure, and create a governance adapted to its growth.

### The Role and Activities of UNESCO

On 20 October 2005, all 191 member states of the United Nations Educational, Scientific and Cultural Organization (UNESCO) adopted the Convention on the Protection and Promotion of Diversity of Cultural Expression, the influence of which on Europe is clearly visible in the orientation of the strategies regarding the external relations of the European Union, as well as in the European Agenda for Culture. It constitutes a reference for European strategy in cultural affairs.

This convention was ratified by the European Community and came into force in March 2007. It recognizes the uniqueness of cultural activities, goods and services, invested as they are with value and meaning – hence the right for states to evolve policies to favour the cultural sector on the understanding that the European position excludes the audiovisual sector from engaging in commercial negotiations, this right possibly being challenged due to commitments to liberalize the market. The convention also encourages more international cultural exchanges, providing opportunities for the developing countries.

Protocols for cultural cooperation concern South America, India, Canada, Central America, the countries around the Mediterranean and South-East Asia. The UNESCO convention is thus right at the heart of cultural cooperation: existing agreements and protocols include arrangements for the travel opportunities of artists, live performance, publishing, the protection of cultural heritage and monuments, as well as film, radio and television.

In the audiovisual sector, there is a case for enabling the negotiation and implementation of national co-production agreements, ensuring the promotion of works from partner countries, granting preferential terms for countries where the audiovisual industry is not so developed and scheduling measures for financial support to the developing countries.

For music, the priorities are the creation of programmes of exchanges between European and foreign music ensembles, the setting up of institutions to facilitate training and exchanges for music professionals (particularly for younger artists), the promotion of programmes defining the practical details of exhibitions by artists from partner countries in festivals and of initiatives favouring the promotion of musical artists, and support for the presence of musicians in international professional events, together with developing exhibitions of work from partner countries in a digital world.

In the world of book publishing, the main programmes are to support translations, the supply of books and the acquisition of library stocks in developing countries, support for the development of local publishing, co-publishing and the transfer of intellectual rights between local and European publishers, training sessions for publishers and booksellers and the organizing of festivals, fairs and literary events.

As for live performance, it is a case of promoting the meetings between professionals: exchanges and training, including participating in auditions and the expansion and promotion of networks. Also envisaged are such things as developing co-productions, encouraging cooperation regarding technical standards and promoting the works of third countries (including the translation and publishing of plays for the theatre, organizing public readings and live performances, setting up festivals and developing artist residencies).

Priority would be given in the fine arts to promoting artists and their work through exhibitions and festivals, inviting artists and practitioners in the European Union, and creating specific networks and sites to develop these arts in the countries concerned.

Traditional and folk arts are significant activities and are seen as important by many developing countries.

To be sustainable, there is a case for ensuring two-way cultural frameworks of cooperation with existing European Community programmes and arrangements. Thus, the Culture 2007–13 Programme, endowed with a €400 million budget and mainly aimed at intra-Community initiatives, also welcomes cooperation with third countries. During the period 2007–9, projects have targeted India and China, with

Brazil in 2008–10. The €15 million *Media Mundus* programme, adopted on 21 October for the period 2010–13, funds audiovisual projects undertaken jointly by professionals from the European Community and third countries. In the same way, in the Europe-Mediterranean region, *Euromed Heritage IV* (2008–12) encourages participation by the local populations in their own cultural heritage, *Euromed III* (2009–12) aims to stimulate audiovisual cooperation, and the Anna Lindh Foundation, co-financed by the European Union, supports the development of dialogue between cultures.

These agreements for cultural cooperation are related to the main thrust of external aid. The €11.6 million 2007–13 European Neighbourhood and Partnership Instrument (ENPI)[8] supports cooperation in the promotion of multicultural dialogue, the preservation of historic and cultural heritage and the exploitation of its development potential.

The Tenth European Development Fund plans to spend €21.3 million out of the total €22.7 billion budget for the period 2008–13on culture, including social and cultural development, training, housing and health. The €16.9 billion fund for Development Cooperation includes a €50 million programme (2007–13) – *Investing in People* – for access to local culture and for the safeguarding and promotion of cultural diversity. The €172 million 2007–13 fund for Cooperation with Industrialized and Other High-Income Countries and Territories aims particularly at promoting the links between peoples, with education and training programmes.

### The Priorities of Cultural and Scientific Diplomacy: The Role of the Ministry for European and Foreign Affairs

The present priorities for French cultural and scientific diplomacy are the promotion of French expertise internationally, the perspective of European development policy, strategies for supporting rural and urban development and boosting French film and broadcasting abroad. The global thrust of this diplomacy is for knowledge, development support, growth and the Millennium Development Goals – seeking opportunities

---

[8]  Operational since 1 January 2007 (when it replaced the *Tacis* cooperation programme for Eastern European countries and the similar *Meda* for the Mediterranean countries), it is the main source of funding for the seventeen partner countries (ten Mediterranean countries, six countries of Eastern Europe and Russia).

for a French world digital presence and putting creativity at the heart of foreign cultural initiatives.

*French Expertise International*[9] is a powerful focus for French cultural and scientific diplomacy.[10] World demand for expertise is currently a question of influence, representing an important market in the political, economic, scientific, technological and cultural sectors. The same applies to research and development and to training and teaching. To this end, the *Direction générale de la mondialisation, du développement et des partenariats* has drawn up a strategic framework document in consultation with all the key players: the goal is to bring together the necessary tools to mobilize the promotion of French expertise. Some questions could be: what mechanisms should be developed to keep an alert and to respond to the calls for tender from international fund providers, how to identify pools of experts, and what improvements are needed in the functioning and coordinating of new and existing tools so as to advance the position of French expertise internationally? This strategic document has six main thrusts:

- research and higher education with educational and linguistic cooperation;

- artistic, audiovisual and cultural engineering, including heritage;

- the rule of law and governance;

- the environment and sustainable development;

- the economy; and

- business and the private sector: the promotion of an environment favouring investment and economic development.

The draft strategy document, proposed to all in the cultural and scientific network, receives proposals and operational recommendations for a better understanding of the needs of sponsors, foreign governments and other fund providers – optimizing and coordinating an alert regarding

---

[9] <www.fei.gouv.fr/>.

[10] On this, see, for example, <http://www.ambafrance-de.org/spip.php?recherche=Fren ch+Expertise+International+is+a+powerful+focus+for+French+cultural+and+scientific+ diplomacy.&Submit=Ok&id_secteur=2&page=recherche> and the work of Pierre Bühler, Director of *France Coopération internationale*.

calls for tender and a capacity for responses that are rapid, professional and competitive and based on an accurate identification of the availability of experts.

*Les perspectives de la politique européenne de développement* raise the question, by how much European aid and bilateral aid complement one another within the framework of a permanent dialogue with the European Commission – in Brussels and at the local level. French strategy and European policies for development, the main institutional issues of the Lisbon Treaty of 1 December 2009, provide opportunities for synergies between European aid and bilateral aid. There are as many objectives as there are opportunities for France in the post-Lisbon context. The main French strategic concerns regarding European development policy have been adopted by the *Comité interministériel de la coopération internationale et du développement* (*Cicid*), in conjunction with the French framework document on cooperation. This strategy follows from the acknowledgement of the importance of European channels in the transmission of French aid: in excess of 23 per cent of French public aid to development in 2009, representing over half the number of the donations – the impact and visibility of which are questioned, often by French members of parliament. This French strategy will be followed by an action plan aimed at putting the French process into working order to provide more impetus – from the debate of ideas to the granting of the European funds.

For its part, the European Commission published in late 2010 a Green Paper on the future of European development policy. Of particular significance is the importance given to social and employment policies, to the place of women in society and to local authorities, taking into account the specifics of each developing country for the granting of aid.

*La stratégie pour l'aide au développement territorial et urbain* is an important strand of French diplomacy and it concerns directly the significance of the local community and the challenges posed by urban growth in the developing countries. It considers decentralization and resource planning development as tools of public policy closer to the citizen and a strengthening of state measures, urban governance at the heart of the fight against the urban–rural divide, and achieving the Millennium Development Goals.

The main issues are linked to the rapid growth of cities. The rate of urban population growth will double by 2050, especially in the developing countries. Such urbanization certainly brings development such as access to services, but it also risks the construction of shanty towns along with social and environmental tensions. The territorial approach thus offers a suitable framework for democratic governance by creating 'areas of trust' to encourage the representatives of local authorities to allow participation and ownership and to promote more integrated sectoral policies. This is an essential role of the *Agence française de développement*, notably in an urban context, aiming as it does at a global approach to project management for local authorities to promote improvements to living conditions, urban productivity and planning, in the wider public interest. It is important to use all these means to bring a coherent approach for territorial projects carried out by the community, such as job creation, social project management and the protection of the environment. The Agency systematically looks for synergies with the French stakeholders for urban cooperation, particularly with that which is decentralized, such as the implementation of pilot studies and the strengthening of capacity. It has become necessary to think beyond a purely technical approach to urban development. Each city has a history, a mix of economic and social functions, and, for its citizen, a necessity – which should evolve into a desire – to live together. Integrated urban development should combine all these dimensions under public authority control and take into account the problems of settlement, density and land management strategies. We must then seek a renewed policy for urbanism, based on a partnership approach and the processes of urban governance. We can take as an example the *Partenariat français pour la ville et les territoires*, which encourages the coming together of those involved in urban planning cooperation across France to bring to the international debate a common vision centred on reinforcing political project supervision and a wish to live together to promote local democracy and a social mix. Urban planners and the French private sector can also contribute implementation methods – legal provisions and urban planning – to further this political vision.

*L'audiovisuel extérieure de la France* is an ever-evolving sector and the speed of change in the audiovisual industries around the world is significant, as is the emergence of new players, including, notably, China (which has invested heavily in the development of four international television channels, including the francophone CCTV-F), India, Brazil and Venezuela. The French regional information channel Africa 24 was started in 2004. The audiovisual landscape is thus characterized by intense competition between 27,000 channels, 5,000 of which are available in Europe and 750 in the Arab countries, and by three discontinuities: the end of analogue transmissions and the growth of digital methods, the need felt by many nations for an offering more linked to identity, and the emergence of new avenues of reception for the new generation. It is necessary therefore to have a presence in all media formats and to adapt content, keeping pace with Euronews, France 24, TV5 Monde and RFI. An example could be, say, texting in Hausa – one of the main commercial languages of Africa – for health counselling.

At the same time, new constraints appear, such as the steep rise in charges for sport transmission rights. For example, the cost of rights to the African Nations Football Cup have risen twentyfold. Distribution payments for the cable operators and the necessity to negotiate inch by inch with access providers and content aggregators, such as the provision of television channels to hotels, must be kept in mind. In spite of this very competitive context, the development of various private and public operators is growing. In two years, RFI and, notably, its Arabic language subsidiary Radio Monte Carlo Doualiya (MCD) have regained audience figures. And notwithstanding the differences between radio and television, RFI's expertise in Africa proved very useful to France 24. By the end of 2010, it was growing in effect on the social networks. TV5 Monde has 210 million homes linked by cable or satellite as well as 8.6 million site visits a month on the Internet, and its audience grew by 2.5 per cent in 2009, owing in part to the start of its Pacific transmissions, and to subtitling. There are many synergies between France 24 and RFI, such as audience surveys, common calls for tender and channels of distribution.

*Euronews* sets multilingualism at the heart of its strategy, giving it a reach of 330 million homes in 153 countries. Its audience in Europe is greater than that of CNN.

Independently from radio and television channels, France exports its telecasts and its expertise with varying success, enjoying excellent results with animation, but less so in drama.

## Scientific Cooperation

The 'diplomacy of knowledge' deals with global issues. And scientific cooperation fulfils the French objectives of influence and of development in partner countries. Scientific culture, the debate of ideas, higher education, expertise and research are the many partnerships with the relevant ministries and institutions that work towards the development of an image in science and technology for France. The specific objectives of this diplomacy of knowledge are:

- to back the internationalization and economic development of research, as well as the dissemination of French science and technology cultures;

- to turn science to advantage for diplomatic initiatives;

- to strengthen relations between societies; and

- to create diplomatic posts to support scientific cooperation, both multilateral and multi-partnership.

The emergence of this concept of the diplomacy of knowledge shows the growing interdependency of science and diplomacy in forming French foreign policy. This diplomatic approach aims at strengthening the influence and attractiveness of the countries implementing it, at promoting credible answers to global issues and at stimulating public debate and scientific education for better involvement of the social players. A diplomacy of research thus takes on its full meaning when it effects transnational mobilization, a political support to further scientific cooperation and to define priorities and mutual strengths to help resolve global problems.

What is at stake is the construction of a citizenship based on knowledge, supported by school education and media coverage of scientific learning. *Universcience* was established on 1 January 2010 when the *Cité des Sciences et de l'Industrie* merged with the *Palais de la Découverte*. With Claudie Haigneré as president, it contributes to the international diffusion of science and technology culture, and it intends to enhance its involvement, with priority given to national structures, particularly where the dissemination of French as a scientific language is concerned.

The national science academies network, which is in the order of 130, is another particularly important initiative. In this respect, the hands-on attitude appears a novel method of education, appealing to the creativity of the students – to real experience as opposed to the mere accumulation of knowledge.

Another essential field is the necessary evolution of a North–South scientific dialogue. These partnerships between universities or with research organizations must contribute to political decisions regarding development. New tools and practices must be developed, particularly at the request of partners from the South in order to favour large measures of multilateral funding, long-term partnerships and the co-funding and co-piloting of initiatives. Faced with these realignments of partnership, the *Institut de recherche pour le développement* (IRD) was invested with a new governance to develop internally a funding agency with a programming role with which other operators will enter into partnership: the *Agence inter-établissements de recherche pour le développement* (AIRD).

Finally, the diplomacy of knowledge prioritizes three guidelines:

- the development of international partnerships respecting the autonomy and responsibilities of research organizations and universities grouped into large centres, *Pôles de recherche et d'enseignement supérieur* (Pres), for the internationalization of French research as advanced by the Ministry for Higher Education and Research;

- the emerging of new players nationally, including the five alliances which cover each of the priorities in research and innovation and which will have the ability to respond rapidly to international calls for tender; and

- a strengthening, through various incentives, particularly fiscal, for innovation allowing the production and export of goods and services stemming from research.

*Aid to Development* and the *Millennium Development Goals* face many cultural and scientific challenges – the need to take into account world state assets, the quality of growth and human development on a global scale marked by major issues, a collective and consistently evolving European governance, the G20 and the arrival of new actors.[11]

In this connection it is important to note a White Paper, the Policy Framework Paper of Cooperation to Development, which brings together the ministries in charge of international cooperation, the *Agence française*

[11] See Catherine Aubertin and Franck-Dominique Vivien (eds), *Le développement durable*, new edn. (Paris: La Documentation française, 2010).

*du développement* and civil society. This answers the need to adapt and project the strategy of cooperation of France in a world facing global problems, new arrivals such as the emerging markets, local and regional authorities and non-governmental organizations. French diplomacy has always sought checks and balances from globalization – to be fair and sustainable, subject to the meeting of universal needs and the recognition of human rights. This White Paper has four major thrusts for cooperation: crisis prevention and management; support for fair and sustainable economic growth; the fight against poverty; and the protection of state assets throughout the world. Four priority geographic areas are targeted: sub-Saharan Africa, the Mediterranean countries, emerging markets, and states experiencing instability.

In this sense, the Millennium Development Goals place human development at the heart of economic growth: successes in schooling, the reduction of pandemics and access to water must be realized. In the last ten years, new challenges have appeared: global warming, the maintenance of peace, demographic issues, migration, energy, food and the financial crisis. In New York, during September 2010, France reaffirmed its strong commitment to realizing the Millennium Development Goals before 2015, and has emphasized shared responsibilities, green growth and solidarity, democratic governance, respect for world state assets and the promoting of innovative financial initiatives. As in France, the European Union came up with a Green Paper on a European strategy of cooperation and development, reaffirming the importance of cohesiveness for all policies within the confines of the European Union.

## Digital Development

Digital Development constitutes an essential tool of a diplomacy of influence. It is undoubtedly the main avenue for the exchange of information, knowledge, culture, film and television. It also brings risks of too great a concentration of power – and choice of content – in too few hands. Indeed, the influence wielded associated with the rapid growth of digital methods is cause for concern. Advances in technology ideally should be harnessed to serve French cultural diplomacy, against intense competition from other industrialized or emergent countries. During the *Journées du réseau français à l'étranger 2010*, Nathalie Kosciusko-Morizet, then Secretary of State for Research and Development of the Digital Economy, underlined the role of the cultural and scientific network for intercultural dialogue. Digital methods should also help France to uphold its values and engage with the challenges of globalization. It is a widely held view in France that the French language does not have the presence it should on the Internet. The absence of a common European digital market and the constraints imposed by inconsistencies between each state's own laws on digital rights hinder the development of cultural services online. The challenge, thus, is to give firm support to French players by changing the regulatory framework and rendering them significant assistance, as will be done with the *Grand Emprunt*[12] or 'National Loan'. Also significant is the French perspective on Internet governance, insisting particularly on a right to anonymity and respect for privacy.

Dominique Wolton stated during these *Journées*, that the digital offer is ever growing, saying that after the present build-up of infrastructure we will meet resistance among Internet users which will tend to work against cultural diversity. No combination of technology can replace a human network. In this sense, creativity must be at the heart of French cultural initiatives: this is a top priority. The cultural influence of France around the world relies on its creators. The demand for culture has never been so strong, judging by the worldwide success of artists, architects, creators and relevant companies. This is the challenge facing the new cultural agency. The *Institut français* will need to respond, faced with this 'appetite for France' – or, rather, with the diverse demands emanating from various regions of the world and spawned by the cultural network. As Xavier Darcos, president of the *Institut français*, underlines forcefully:

> to fight against standardization, cultural imperialism and loss of identity [...] against the tendency to uniformity of artistic and cultural production, creation, critical thinking, and the acquisition and exchange of knowledge, relationships with others must form the backbone of France's foreign cultural policy.

[12] The 'National Loan', presented by President Sarkozy on 22 June 2010, provides for 'a creative digital France, building a high-speed broadband network for all, ensuring data centres are efficient, with distance healthcare allowing the aged to stay at home, developing virtual services, capitalizing on HD [high-definition] culture'.

# 4

# Cultural Diplomacy and the Arts

Cultural assets and services enjoy values which cannot be reduced to a mere economic figure. In this area, the commitment of France is one of mutual cultural exchange between countries, acknowledging the European dimension of these partnerships, and a declaration of solidarity between cultures.

The cultural network abroad and the *Institut français* cultural agency both aim at reinforcing the circulation of ideas and works, at encouraging mutual knowledge and understanding, through projects based on common commitments: it is then a question of harnessing French cultural and intellectual creativity with all partner countries by promoting the cultural and audiovisual industries, as well as organizing debates on controversial themes in society, such as immigration, bioethics and secularity.[1]

In arts and culture, the *Direction générale de la mondialisation, du développement et des partenariats* (DGM) of the Ministry of Foreign and European Affairs, working in consultation with the Ministry for Culture and Communication, benefits from the expertise of the foreign cultural agency, the *Institut français*. Furthermore, it can count on a wide network of cultural services, cultural establishments and *Alliances françaises*.[2]

At the heart of international artistic exchanges, the *Département des échanges et coopérations artistiques* of the *Institut français* provides expertise and artistic counselling to many partners around the world. It is

---

[1] For the activities of the cultural and scientific network, see <www.latitudefrance. org>.

[2] On the importance of business sponsorship, see <www.admical.org/editor/files/ Enquete_ADMICAL-CSA_2010web.pdf>.

assigned to assist in the finding of film locations in France, Africa and the Caribbean, to develop projects by theme and a multidisciplinary approach to programming, and to respond to events to maximize advantage for the artistic stage in various disciplines. It can accompany international tours of shows and exhibitions within the framework of exchanges with foreign museums and partners. It also devises, in dialogue with the organizers and the partners of the events, the artistic planning of foreign cultural seasons in France.

Through calls for projects, this department also contributes support to many programmes it does not itself initiate, and responds to queries for support to partners in the professions – artists, companies, the French cultural network and the stage abroad – as regards cooperation and distribution. These calls for projects are made each March and October, and are assessed by a committee of French professionals.

This department is organized around two functions: one is the production of grand international biennial events and other ambitious operations, in concert with international partners; the other concerns artistic and cultural circulation, exchange and training – by promoting diverse independent projects.

### The Performing Arts, the Visual Arts and Architecture: Key Sectors of Cultural Diplomacy

The dissemination of contemporary creativity in all its forms is a priority for the international artistic policy of France. Examples of foreign operations include: 'Baltic Sounds French' for contemporary music; 'France Danse' for contemporary ballet; 'Paris Calling', in London, for contemporary art; and 'Berlin–Paris', in Germany, and 'Croisements' (Encounters), in China, for the exchange of works of art. In France, there are the 'Focus' platforms, organized to find locations for large cultural events, such as theatre and the visual arts.

The implementation of cultural diversity is the second priority and implies the embracing of another country's cultural wealth as well as the promotion of French culture abroad. 'Cross Years' festivals in China and Brazil recently have allowed the co-organizing of many events in the artistic, scientific, educational and economic spheres. In return, 'foreign cultural seasons' in France disseminate the creativity of the guest country.

Since the first, in 1985 for India, they have encouraged the discovery of the diverse cultural aspects of many countries.

Improvements in professional standards within the artistic channels of countries in the *Zone de solidarité prioritaire* (ZSP) are focused upon enabling better access to national and international markets, stressing the economic value of culture, and taking the form of large themed events in Africa and the Caribbean. These are conceived as professional platforms, such as the biennial *Danse l'Afrique Danse*, the *Rencontres de Bamako*, the *Biennale Danses Caraïbes* and *L'Afrique est à la mode* in the search for new market territories.[3]

The European dimension of cultural and artistic cooperation is represented by the European Network of Cultural Institutes (EUNIC). In May 2007, the European Commission published its European Agenda, with three main goals: cultural diversity and intercultural dialogue; culture as a catalyst of creativity; and culture as an essential element of international relations.[4] At the Brussels meeting of the heads of European Union external cultural relations in September 2010, two main priorities were proposed: to take into consideration in the 'European Union 2020' strategy the potential of culture in matters of creativity and innovation (notably through support for cultural enterprises) and to recognize the role of culture in the fight against poverty and social exclusion. Other priorities included the strategic goals of the European Agenda for Culture 2007–13, the adoption of a label for European Heritage (a French initiative) and the digitization of film theatres, taking into consideration the complete chain of audiovisual creation: development, production and distribution. The talks have yet to evolve into concrete recommendations issued to the member states.

Performing arts include street arts, circus, ballet, theatre, puppetry and music – contemporary, ancient, classical and current.

---

[3] Defined by the French Government in February 1998, the *Zone de solidarité prioritaire* (ZSP) comprises the less-developed countries with which France intends forging strong partnerships to promote solidarity and sustainable development. The ZSP countries are: Afghanistan (provisionally), Algeria, Angola, Benin, Burkina Faso, Burundi, Cambodia, Cameroon, Cape Verde, Central African Republic, Chad, Comoros, Congo, Cuba, Democratic Republic of Congo, Djibouti, Dominican Republic, Eritrea, Ethiopia, Gabon, Ghana, Gambia, Guinea, Guinea-Bissau, Haiti, Ivory Coast, Kenya, Laos, Lebanon, Liberia, Madagascar, Mali, Mauritania, Morocco, Mozambique, Namibia, Niger, Nigeria, Palestinian Territories, Ruanda, São Tomé and Principe, Senegal, Sierra Leone, South Africa, Sudan, Surinam, Tanzania, Togo, Tunisia, Uganda, Vanuatu, Vietnam, Yemen and Zimbabwe.

[4] See <http://ec.europa.eu/culture>.

Circus arts constitute a new sphere of foreign cultural activity for France, one which has acquired an international reputation.[5] This is how, in 2009, the 'Polo Circo', or Circus Centre, was created in Buenos Aires, in partnership with several French regional and local authorities, which facilitated the travel of about 100 artists and circus professionals from France. This permanent artistic centre created by the Argentine city authorities takes the form of five marquees erected on six hectares of land entirely dedicated to the circus arts.

For its first circus festival, from 26 June to 5 July 2009, the city of Buenos Aires had chosen to build its entire programme around French artistic experience: the Aïtal Circus, the Nadir, the 'Armo (*Atelier de Recherche en Manipulation d'Objets*)-Jérôme Thomas' company, 'Morosof', 'Un loup pour l'homme', 'Non Nova', the *Centre national des arts du cirque* and the *École nationale des arts du cirque* of Rosny sous Bois.

By 2010, French expertise still played a major role in the programme, with several companies contributing – 'L'Attraction celeste', the 'Petit Travers' collective, 'Bang Bang' circus, Laurent Bigot's 'Petit Cirque', 'O Ultimo Momento' company, the Rosny sous Bois school and the *Studios du Cirque* from Marseilles. This dynamic of young circus talents is well recognized internationally and is in great demand. The same applies to the street arts. Royal de Luxe', 'La Machine' and 'Groupe F' are prestigious companies, invited to every continent. In June 2009, the giant mechanical spiders of 'La Machine' strolled around the streets of Yokohama, Japan for five days to celebrate the harbour's 150th anniversary. Invited by Michelle Bachelet, President of Chile, the giant puppets of 'Royal de Luxe' attracted nearly two million people in the streets of Santiago to open the country's bicentennial celebrations of independence in January 2010. The firework displays of 'Groupe F' illuminated the skies of London on New Year's Eve 2009, also inaugurating the Burj Khalifa, the tallest building in the world, in Dubai, and opening the celebrations of 'Istanbul, European Capital of Culture' in January 2010.

These companies also take part in extended French events abroad, such as 'Groupe F' in Rio de Janeiro for the inauguration of the French season in Brazil and the closing, in April 2010, of 'Bonjour India', a French cultural festival in that country.[6]

5  See <www.cnac.fr/page_accueil.php?rec=25>.
6  Source: <www.diplomatie.gouv.fr>.

Hip-hop is another domain particularly acknowledged outside France, with many artists including Mourad Merzouki ('Käfig' company) and Kader Attou ('Accrorap').

French ballet has also met success internationally over the last thirty years. While choreographers Angelin Preljocaj, Philippe Decouflé and Maguy Marin have been well received for many years, others, notably Jérôme Bel and Boris Charmatz,have also gained an international reputation. The great ballets of the Paris and Lyon opera theatres often embark on international tours, recently to Australia, China and Russia. These tours are jointly funded from private sources (with fundraising organized by the French diplomatic service and local cultural institutions) and state sources (from French ministries and international organizations).

One must not underestimate the impact of large-scale productions such as 'France Danse' for French ballet, in partnership with the cultural institutions in the countries involved. Major business organizations, cultural institutions, cultural cooperation services in the French embassies and the *Departement des échanges et coopérations artistiques* make it possible to mount such ambitious productions and tours.

Cooperation in the field of training is provided by the *Conservatoire itinérant de danse classique et contemporaine*, a programme working around the world with the support of the cultural services in French embassies.

At an international level, the stage is perceived through theatre directors of world fame, such as Pascal Chéreau, Ariane Mnouchkine and Peter Brook, together with a new generation of directors and playwrights such as Olivier Py, Eric Vignier and Joël Pommerat. These operations can take the form of large-scale events supported by major institutions. The *Comédie Française*, France's national theatres and companies such as the *Théâtre du soleil* regularly go on international tours, where they stage the best of their repertoires. In 2010, the *Comédie Française* completed a tour of Russia for the France-Russia 'Cross-Years' festival.

Cooperation can also take the form of projects in various formats around contemporary creativity and artistic renewal. Thus, plays by Philippe Quesne and Joël Pommerat are in great demand. Hungary, Belgium, the United Kingdom and North America for Quesne in 2010. Russia, Poland, Ireland and Canada for Pommerat in that same year.

As in the other artistic fields, the *Institut français* has conceived a platform to talent-spot and promote French theatre, presenting the latest French scene, *Focus theatre*. This aims at empowering French and foreign professionals, and it offers a framework for the cultural network to organize programmes of invitations to practitioners from outside France. Thus, in 2010, an event was organized with the 'Festival Via' in Maubeuge and Mons to present the latest works f Mathieu Bauer, David Bobée and Xavier Kim, as well as less-well-known authors such as Antoine Defoort, Joachim Latarjet and the GdRA collective.

Promoting French theatre is seen as encouraging the repertoire, dramatic art, today's writers and literature in general. The 'Cross-Years' programme provides an ideal framework for this exercise, but audiences were also able to discover Marie Darieussecq in Iceland and Olivier Cadot in Italy. These events can also be organized for anniversaries, as in Ghent in 2010, or to enrich a publishing or theatre event, as with Marguerite Duras in New York that same year.

The French music industry must confront the dual challenges of the economic crisis and piracy. As the market has experienced a contraction in recent years, export is seen as vital for those involved. French musicians are very active internationally, with record numbers of concerts and new albums. One French CD in three is sold outside of France, and for some record labels export sales can represent over half of their turnover.[7]

Facing an international crisis affecting every market, the four priorities for the French music industry are the United States, Germany, the United Kingdom and Japan. For the first time, in 2010, the *Bureau export de la musique française* proposed a plan of support to the music channels for their digital development abroad by providing finance for digital projects such as Web promotion tools, the adaptation of Internet sites and commercial campaigns, together with proposing a market-alert service and a business-to-business initiative with the digital actors in the main countries in the market.

## The French Music Export Market in 2009

Export turnover in 2009 for CDs was €45.2 million, with classical music representing 20 per cent compared with only 7.5 per cent in the domestic

---

[7] Source: 'bureau export' <http://french-music.org>.

market.[8] Composer royalties levied by the *Société des auteurs compositeurs et éditeurs de musique (Sacem)*[9] from exports amounted to €77.7 million, with direct levies on music publishers from exports at €12 million. Total turnover for exports from the French music industry, excluding the performing arts, was €134.9 million. Sales in Europe accounted for 73 per cent, including 22 per cent for the Benelux countries, 15 per cent for Germany and 13 per cent for Switzerland and Austria. The Americas represented 15.6 per cent, Asia 7.6 per cent, including 5.5 per cent for Japan, and Oceania 2.6 per cent. The Export Bureau granted a total of €3 million to professional French musicians.

Music is in constant evolution, and numerous talents emerge each year. Groups such as 'Moriarty' and 'Cocoon' have blossomed on the international scene with the aesthetic power of their stage presence. International audiences gave an excellent reception to the electronic music of David Guetta, who received a Grammy award in 2010, and also to the pop-rock sung in English of 'Phoenix', 'M83' and 'Plastiscines', the hard rock of 'Gojira', the colourful pop of 'Sliimy', and the *Made in France* world music of Amadou and Mariam and of Yael Naïm.

The electronic scene and French song meet with renewed interest on the international stage, due to a new musical identity, like Laurent Garnier and 'Birdy Nam Nam', and a new generation of interpreters, including Jeanne Cherhal and Coralie Clément.

There is a special place for jazz. The United States, Italy and France are the three proactive countries of this musical genre, which increasingly finds a market abroad. In the same way, the many French festivals build sustainable relations with their foreign counterparts.

Classical music is also diverse and large companies of musicians, such as 'Les Arts florissants' and 'Les Musiciens du Louvre', continue to have an important role as do the other musical interpreters 'Les Talens Lyriques' and the 'Ensemble Matheus'. Younger players count 'La Chapelle Rhénane' and the 'Pygmalion' ensemble in their number. If Baroque music has been

---

[8] Source: <http://french-music.org>. 'Les chiffres clés 2009–2010', after Syndicat national de l'édition phonographique, Union des producteurs phonographiques français indépendants, Sacem, Chambre syndicale de l'édition musicale, bureauexport.

[9] *Société des auteurs compositeurs et éditeurs de musique*, a non-profit organization managed by the creators and publishers of music, protecting, representing and serving the interests of the authors, composers and publishers of music.

rediscovered, then classical and pre-romantic music has also benefited from the growing activity of these quality ensembles.

Contemporary music is represented by the one permanent company, the 'Ensemble Intercontemporain', directed by Susanna Mälkki, but new ensembles like 'Court-Circuit' manage to maintain their artistic position in a sector always in demand abroad.

French orchestras are very active. In addition to the *Orchestre national de France*, the *Orchestre de Paris*, the *Philharmonique* of Radio France and the regional orchestras have a considerable presence abroad thanks to the financial commitment of French regional and local authorities, and the same applies to more recently formed companies of musicians such as *La Chambre Philharmonique* and *Les Siècles*. Instrumental soloists of international standing include Gautier Capuçon, Anne Gastinel, Hélène Grimaud, Emmanuel Pahud and Alexandre Tharaud, amongst many others.

The participation of France in an international dialogue for the visual arts is a priority, as is shown clearly in the report submitted by the director of *Arts Paris*, Henri Jobbé-Duval.[10] It promotes an enhanced presence in France of French artistic creativity while providing better preparation and participation for international artistic exchanges – by developing exchanges abroad for French art schools, by broadening and improving the system of residencies and research grants, by facilitating the welcome and hosting of foreign artists and professionals and by developing the participation of their French counterparts in contemporary art. It is vitally necessary better to facilitate the presence of French artists abroad by scaling up cooperation between French and foreign operators, by further encouraging the circulation of private and public collections, by concentrating on innovative subjects and by determining reliable indicators to the presence of French artists abroad as an improvement on the present use of the *Kunst Kompass*[11] indicator of the German newspaper *Das Kapital*.

As early as 2010 and 2011, several proposals in the Jobbé-Duval report have come into effect. This has seen the writing of a *vade mecum* or handbook for the French cultural network and the heads of French

---

[10]    Henri Jobbé-Duval (ed.), *Rapport Jobbé-Duval pour améliorer la participation de la France au dialogue artistique international dans le domaine des arts visuels: propositions issues des ateliers de réflexion* (April–July 2008), Ministère des Affaires étrangères et européennes, Ministère de la Culture et de la Communication, Paris, July 2008.

[11]    The *Compass of the Arts*, created in 1970 by Willy Bongard, a German economist, rates the reputations of the 100 most popular artists in the world.

institutions, specifying all the tools available for the promotion of French creativity abroad. Identifying those larger projects supported by French institutions is important so as to be able to consider, at an early stage, their international development, as is supporting and making more sustainable several earlier initiatives such as 'Paris Calling' in London, 'Paris–Los Angeles' and 'Berlin–Paris' – programmes in which museums, galleries and art centres collaborate closely. Consolidating the public–private partnership has seen bilateral awards and funds bring together state sponsors with private donors such as the Cartier Fondation, Guerlain and Louis Vuitton.

Great contemporary art encounters take place in France and maintain a high visibility. These include the *Foire internationale de l'art contemporain* (*Fiac*), *Arts Paris*, *Paris Phot*, *Biennale de Lyon* and *Rencontres d'Arles* (formerly *Rencontres internationales de la photographie d'Arles*). In the same vein, the return of artists of international repute to French art galleries bears witness to a new dynamism in international dialogue.

Many innovative places for contemporary art have been created in recent years – arts centres, artists' collectives, residencies and exhibition spaces – along with the development of digital arts, which brings on a new generation of artists whose work is firmly interdisciplinary, such as photography and video.

Aesthetic industrial design work today provides an innovative perspective while drawing firmly on tradition and savoir-faire. The *Institut français* assists designers for major international shows such as World Design Capitals together with numerous 'designer week' and 'designer month' events throughout the world:

- It supports regional activities within France which have an international dimension, such as the *Cité du Design* in Saint Etienne.

- It operates through a joint programme with the major manufacturing industries, such as Sèvres, Gobelins and furniture makers and helps to spread French 'savoir faire' internationally.

- It encourages the activities and educational achievements of schools that specialize in design and graphics.

- It commissions mobile modular units capable of being used internationally to promote the French cultural network abroad in such things as basic design, graphic design, technological innovation, tableware and crafts.

- It promotes the distribution of examples of good design for foreign national collections.

Also important is the development of digital creativity. Digital arts have their own characteristics: they enrich other disciplines, including dance, theatre, the visual arts, stage performance and music. Their convergence with other digital practices provides a wealth of innovation and exploration for the most active multidisciplinary artists today. The *Institut français* has a policy of promoting digital development through professional networks, collaborating with Digital Arts Network in the co-publication of a specialist reference book on the subject and promoting an international network of major world specialist events such as the Digital Month in Tokyo and BIAN in Montreal.

In collaboration with the Ministry of Culture and Communication and with French art magazines, the *Institut français* has helped to create a 'digital kiosk' for the translation and dissemination of a regular selection of texts by art critics and historians. It supports innovative events for experimental film and video. It produces videos which can be distributed through the French cultural network abroad, such as the *Centre National des Arts Plastiques* (CNAP) collection of experimental film and video and a DVD production of audiovisual works from the *École Nationale Supérieure des Arts Décoratifs* (ENSAD), together with *IFmapp*, a web resource for the use of artists and other professionals. It promotes links between the arts and sciences by producing modules for the French cultural network abroad, bringing together of art, science and technology.

## Book Publishing Policy:
## The Debate of Ideas, Science and Knowledge

Book publishing is the major cultural industry in France.[12] Exports represent one-quarter of the turnover of French publishing, the country's second greatest export in value after objets d'art in the cultural sector,

---

[12] See <www.diplomatie.gouv.fr/fr/IMG/pdf/Promouvoir-No2-FR-PP-2.pdf>.

respectively €622.9 million and €1,050.3 million in 2008 coming from international sales.[13]

In promoting books abroad, French cultural diplomacy also encourages artistic and cultural production, French scientific expertise and the debate of ideas. This support takes the form of several programmes managed by the *Institut français*: the *Programme d'aide à la publication* (PAP), the *Plan traduire*, the projects of the *Zone de solidarité prioritaire* and the *Fonds d'Alembert* (see below).

Translation promotes awareness of France in the evolution of its intellectual debates and literary creativity: the country's weight of influence is at stake through the medium of books, magazines and websites as vital windows on culture. The *Programme traduction* consists of two parts: PAP supports foreign publishers which make a long-term commitment to publishing French or francophone authors in all spheres. Since its creation in 1990, 18,000 titles have been published in seventy-five different countries. Each programme is named after a personality who has worked for French literature, such as Pushkin in Russia, Burgess in the United Kingdom and Garcia Lorca in Spain. This programme essentially comprises two parts: purchasing the transfer of rights, financed by the central funds of the *Institut français*, and supporting foreign publishers, financed through the French diplomatic service.

The *Plan traduire* was created in 2005 and complements the publishing programme. It aims at training a new generation of translators and creating new databases of translations: *Frenchbooknews* for English, *Tradarab* for Arabic, *Fu Lei* for Chinese and *Librosdefrancia* for Spanish. It compiles databases on the French books already translated in one of the target languages of English, Arabic, Chinese, Spanish or Russian: titles, authors, publishers and translators. This plan also seeks to offer books, magazines and selected articles to translators from the French in these five linguistic zones. Last, in France and abroad, it seeks to enhance the expertise of translators by organizing training sessions and sojourns in France.

Projects in the priority zones for solidarity are a large part of cooperation in book publishing. The promotion of francophone literature from the

---

[13] See Chantal Lacroix, *Statistiques de la culture: chiffres clés 2010; Mini chiffres clés 2010*, ministère de la Culture et de la Communication, Département des études, de la prospective et des statistiques (Deps), Direction de l'information légale et administrative, Paris, 2010.

developing countries of the South is an important issue when defining the future of francophone publishing: the transfer of publishing rights from the North to the South is encouraged, as well as the publishing in their own country of southern authors hitherto exclusively published in France. Co-publishing between publishers of the South is also specifically supported, so as to promote mutual publishing initiatives to achieve better circulation figures.

Cooperation in book publishing thus affects all concerned. Support is offered for national policies for literature and to institutional structures and the circulation of French-language books through local libraries is encouraged. There is support for local publishing through initiatives for such as 'youth' publishers, authors, illustrators, awards and fairs. Aid is provided for the development of bookshops. The *Centre national du livre* (CNL) grants annual funds to help finance the buying of books by French bookshops abroad: up to €330,000 in 2009. The distribution in the developed countries of the North of African literature is supported, as is francophone literature from the South. Modernization is encouraged through the tools of information and communication technology, and efforts are made to exploit the complementary relations between institutional participants and local partners.

The three main book publishing projects are a 'mobilizing' programme named *Edocdev* (*L'écrit et l'accès documentaire au service du développement*); six 'state' projects, mainly located in sub-Saharan Africa, the Maghreb and the Middle East (Burkina Faso, Lebanon, Morocco, Niger, Togo and Tunisia); and an 'inter-state' programme in South-East Asia called *Valease* (*Valorisation de l'écrit en Asie du Sud-Est*) which covers Cambodia, Laos and Vietnam.

Books are closely associated with the debate of ideas – cultural debates, which also benefit from the *Fonds d'Alembert*. This was created in 2002 to promote French intellect and expertise abroad and to promote the debate of ideas. It underwrites conferences, round tables and forums which can be exploited in print and other media. Over seventy projects are thus retained every year to facilitate the organization of meetings between researchers, writers and other personalities in the debate of ideas.

Also noteworthy are the 'Stendhal' missions, a programme created in 1989, enabling authors living in France who have a writing project to have extended visits abroad in order to collect material for their work. The great international book fairs also encourage participation in the international publishing market, with the help of the *Bureau international de l'édition française* (*Bief,* created in 1873 by the *Cercle de la librairie*).

Science offers a growing role for its area of culture in the debate of ideas. Interactive exhibitions, science weeks, scientific film festivals and festivals of science are ideal avenues for its promotion. There is a place for the thirty multi-theme and generalist centres for scientific, technical and industrial culture as resource centres, direct partners with research laboratories, and places of creation and drive. In partnership with French research establishments, they develop science and technology and share this with the public. A good example is the programme for the promotion of science and technology culture in Africa and Madagascar: set up in 2004, its main priority is addressing young people and it is led by the *Institut de recherche pour le développement* in Burkina Faso, Cameroon, the Central African Republic, Chad, Djibouti, Madagascar, Mali, Morocco, Senegal, and Yemen.

Throughout the arts, the impact of digital technology should be appreciated. The *IFVerso* platform of the translated book includes a database of over 70,000 titles translated from French into forty languages and made with locally based collections in partnership with the *Bibliothèque nationale* (French national library) and UNESCO. It is a collaborative and interactive social network for book professionals abroad in the French cultural network together with home-based translators, publishers, editors, those responsible for foreign rights, literary agents, booksellers and academics. It aims to create communities of interest and to promote translations of French books. It also includes a news magazine for specialists in translation.

The Translate Digital Plan and the on-line *Culturethèque* library are two key tools developed for the overseas network of French media libraries. This digital library, classified by country, enables users of such mediatheques to have remote access to various types of digital content, including literature, cinema and music, and contributes to the international visibility of French culture.


## French External Broadcasting

The foreign audiovisual policy of France has evolved considerably since 2008, most notably with the creation of a national authority for programming, *Audiovisuel extérieur de la France* (AEF). This body holds 100 per cent of the shares of *Radio France Internationale* (RFI) and *France 24*, and also 49 per cent of *TV5 Monde*. It operates in a very competitive sector, vital to the influence of France around the world.

The AEF brings together France 24, Monte Carlo Doualiya and RFI. As the premier French international news media group, the AEF broadcasts throughout the world twenty-four hours a day on television, radio, the Internet, mobile phones and tablets. The AEF seeks to develop French influence in the world with a dual francophone and Francophile purpose. Directed by Marie-Christine Saragosse, the AEF currently has a combined weekly audience of over 90 million viewers and listeners, making it the prime international French source – doubling its audience in three years – together with a total of 15.7 million monthly visits on its multimedia platforms (web and mobile).

The AEF budget for 2011 was €330.3 million: €205.1 million for Programme 115, for external broadcasting, and the remainder for Programme 844, to help finance the broadcasting activities of foreign governments.[14] Although this represents an increase of 2.9 per cent of the finance allocated to AEF, stability has yet to be returned to the organization and activities of operators which have, in recent years, encountered significant problems: *TV5 Monde* in 2008, *Radio France Internationale* in 2009 and *France 24* in 2010.

The reason for this is that the broadcasting sector is in a state of flux. *TV5 Monde* has become the second largest network in the world after the MTV music channel.[15] Its weekly audience has now reached 54 million viewers. The launch of the first French 'Web youth' channel, *Tivi5 Monde*, in June 2009, is another step in the direction of young francophone audiences. *France 24* is still enjoying rises in audience figures, notably in the Maghreb and the rest of Africa: it now reaches over 115 million homes. *Arte* continues with its quality offer as a matter of policy, investing in drama and documentaries produced for the Web. *Euronews* has a growing audience and an increase in the choice of languages offered: a Turkish language version was introduced at the beginning of 2010 bringing the total now available to ten. *Radio France Internationale* is a reference

---

[14] M. Didier Mathus, 'Avis présenté au nom de la commission des affaires étrangères sur le projet de loi de finances pour 2011, Média, livre et industries culturelles. Action audiovisuelle extérieure' (14 October 2010).

[15] See <www.tv5.org>.

medium, notably in crisis situations as evinced by its presence during the earthquakes in Haiti.

Of note also is the role of *Canal France International*,[16] a veritable mine of information aimed at attracting buyers from developing countries to French productions, and thus leading to a greater exposure of French programmes.

In spite of today's difficulties, such as the decline of advertising income, terrestrial digital television broadcasting, themed channels and the new media showing a poorer financial return than the old analogue channels, the sales of French radio and television programmes remain buoyant thanks to drama. However, as the Hadas-Lebel report of 2006 showed,[17] the production and distribution of French drama programmes lags behind France's European neighbours. The *Deutsche Welle* and the BBC, for example, invest heavily in their foreign broadcasting. Even just for radio, the contribution of the Foreign and Commonwealth Office helps the BBC to fund an international staff of 4,000 as against the 1,100 for RFI.

During the summer of 2007, the French president announced a reform of the country's foreign broadcasting, to modernize and coordinate its various constituents.

For *TV 5 Monde*, a strategic plan was approved by its financial backers for the 2009–12 period, defining its priorities: these are devising better subtitling; consolidating world distribution by improving audience numbers in the switch to digital; strengthening its multimedia development; and increasing the editorial offer.

At *France 24*, AEF directors have extended broadcasts on the Arabic channel from four to ten hours daily, thanks to economies of scale between *Monte Carlo Doualiya*, the Arabic service of *RFI* and *France 24*.

The modernization of *France 24* is, without doubt, a major challenge in the reform of the external broadcasting service. Stated goals are success in the ratings battle, notably through coverage of the economy and the place of music. A fundamental rethink on languages should strengthen some strategic languages – English, of course, but also the languages of South America and Africa. Radio broadcasts must undergo change – RFI has established a website dedicated to mobile phone use. Modernizing

[16] See <www.cfi.fr/index.php3>.

[17] Raphaël Hadas-Lebel, 'Mission de réflexion et de médiation sur les problèmes relatifs à la rediffusion des fictions françaises sur les chaînes de télévision', Ministry for Culture and Communication, Paris (June 2006).

its management is achieved by regularly reviewing skills and production methods.

The Ministry of Foreign and European Affairs is also heavily involved with the running of the cinema department of the *Institut français*, in charge of the non-commercial distribution of films and documentaries. This is also the case for *Canal France International*, charged with cooperation with the developing countries of the South. The ministry is also represented on the commissions and executive boards of *TV France International* (TVFI) and *Unifrance*.[18] To back these activities, the ministry has a unique network around the world, with fifty audiovisual attachés posted to French embassies. Cooperation is also a major role for both the *Institut national de l'audiovisuel* and the *Centre national du cinema et de l'image animée*.

## Unifrance and the Promotion of French Cinema around the World in Figures

The French film industry ranks second in the world for exports. Two-thirds of productions are exported to at least one other country; new French films average more than one a day on cinema screens around the world; forty French films are broadcast every day on foreign television channels; some 65 million every year watch French films in the cinema – 67.3 million in 2009 – grossing some €350 million of income from foreign film theatres. French cinema is very resilient in its home market, somewhat exceptional for a European country.

In order to promote French feature films each year, *Unifrance* organizes eighty French film festivals, supports sixty international feature film festivals and finances 300 visits abroad for actors and directors.[19] It maintains an international network of 800 distributors – television channel buyers of French films and festival organizers around the world – as well as 1,200 foreign journalists. Each year it organizes 2,500 interviews. The output of the French film industry can be seen in the film theatres of fifty countries and on 200 television channels in thirty countries. Annual support allows some 5,000 short films to be entered for 100 festivals worldwide – 500 films,

---

[18] See <www.tvfrance-intl.com> and <www.unifrance.org>.

[19] Source: <www.unifrance.org/corporate/notre-mission>.

comprising 1,300 distinct copies were selected at 175 festivals in forty-five countries; 100 prizes were awarded for seventy films; and forty-five visits were made by directors and producers; some 200 films were screened by seventeen short film committees. On a technical level, there were sixty selective and forty automatic aids to subtitling.

## World Heritage and Archaeology

To conclude this chapter, we shall stress the importance of world heritage and archaeology, as well as artistic expertise and cultural engineering, in international artistic cooperation.

World Heritage status implies a notion of 'exceptional universal value': each part of the world's heritage is common to all peoples in the world, irrespective of its country or location.[20] Thus, as UNESCO states, each country recognizes that it is the responsibility of the international community to share in the protection of cultural and natural heritage of exceptional and universal value.

Effectively, in the present context of globalization, heritage has become a major political and economic issue. As a measure of the identity of peoples, it can be used to legitimize territorial, political and cultural demands; it can also play a determining role in the development of economic resources or the creation of new employment.

We need to look afresh at the scientific, technical and museum potential at ancient sites, works of art and examples of craftsmanship as candidates for new cultural exchanges.

Archaeology is historically a prime area of cultural diplomacy for France. The Ministry of Foreign and European Affairs finances archaeological activities around the world, together with the publication of the findings, to the tune of €2.66 million in 2011.[21] At the end of December 2010, 150 archaeological digs abroad were approved, including six new sites in Cambodia, Egypt, Ecuador, Iraq and Spain. Criteria of scientific excellence help in evaluating the innovative aspect of research, its contribution to the understanding of the history of the areas concerned, the

[20] See <http://whc.unesco.org>.
[21] For a complete list of sites and documents on archaeology, see <www.diplomatie.gouv.fr/fr/IMG/pdf/Liste_des_missions_2008.pdf>.

training of archaeologists, the strengthening of cultural cooperation and the opportunities for tourism and environmental enhancement of such heritage.

French archaeological research thus supports the restoration of major sites, such as Petra or Jerash (Jordan), or Angkor in Cambodia, where €7.5 million has been invested since 1995. The granting of funds and the activities of research institutes abroad are under the joint authority of the Ministry of Foreign and European Affairs and of the *Centre national de la recherche scientifique* (CNRS). Some 160 archaeological missions are thus undertaking the essential tasks of research and preservation regarding the remains of civilizations and cultures. The cultural heritage they safeguard benefits the host country by contributing to the long-term development of its economy and heritage.

Artistic expertise and cultural engineering are major issues of influence and are integral to cultural cooperation. The main areas of such expertise and engineering are in the performing arts, most notably the circus and street arts, in music, with the rediscovery of ancient examples, in urban festivals such as the *Nuits blanches*, the *Fête de la musique* and the *Folles Journées*. Also covered are festivals and 'French Springs', where foreign seasons in France benefit initially from the extensive network of expertise and studies; in the same way, many festivals, notably in Asia, draw upon artistic expertise led jointly by the cultural services and establishments abroad and the *Institut français*, and for culture and development this means developing local markets with the help of each passing artistic event.

### *Rencontres Malraux:* Discussion Seminars on Cultural Management

French experience in matters of cultural management and policies is of interest to many countries. This has led the Ministry for Culture and Communication to develop cooperation by sending French experts abroad in the most diverse areas of culture.

This is why the *Rencontres Malraux* were created in 1994. Such discussion seminars on cultural management concern countries in the process of reforming their cultural policies and wishing to exploit French experience in cultural management. These seminars last for two or three days and are organized around themes suggested by the host country authorities. They take the form of conferences and debates led by French specialists, aimed at an audience of administrative, political, professional and university leaders. Themes include the organization and logistics of a ministry of culture, decentralization and devolution, state funding of culture, culture legislation, and such specialisms as film policies, heritage conservation, support for artistic creativity and training in the sphere of culture. The organization of the meeting is in the hands of the host country, the French Ministry for Culture making its experts available and covering their travel and subsistence expenses.

If a country wishes *Rencontres Malraux* to be organized, then its ministry of culture or equivalent makes contact with the cultural services of the local French embassy. The application will then be forwarded to the *Département des affaires européennes et internationales* in Paris. At the time of writing, seventy-three *Rencontres Malraux* had been organized in forty-seven countries.[22]

---

[22] These are: Albania (2004), Argentina (1996, 2001), Bahrain (2005), Bosnia and Herzegovina (1997), Brazil (1995, 2009), Bulgaria (2003, 2007) Canada (1997), Chile (1995), China (1998), Colombia (1995, 1997, 2003, 2005), Croatia (2002, 2007), Czech Republic (1998), Dominican Republic (1999), Estonia (2003), Georgia (1999), Guatemala (1998), Hungary (1996, 2004), Iran (2009), Israel (1997, 2000), Italy (1999), Latvia (2008), Lebanon (2002), Lithuania (2001), Macedonia (1997, 2004), Mexico (2004, 2007), Montenegro (2001), Morocco (1995), Norway (2002), Palestine (1995), Panama (2000), Paraguay (1998), Portugal (2008), Romania (two in 2006; 2009), Senegal (1997), Serbia (2007, 2008), Seychelles (2001), Slovakia (2001), South Korea (1996), Spain (2004), Switzerland (2003), Syria (2004), Taiwan (1995, 1996, 2001, two in 2002; 2006, 2008), Thailand (2004), Ukraine (1997, 2005), the United Kingdom (2002), the USA (2008) and Venezuela (1994). Source: <www.culture.gouv.fr/culture/dai/rencmalraux.htm>. This list was updated by the author.

# 5

# Science and University Diplomacy

Research and innovation have played an essential role in the post-war reconstruction of France in areas such as transport, infrastructure, nuclear energy, space exploration and aeronautics.[1] Research and innovation are also the best guarantees for French expertise abroad and offer the greatest potential for science and university cooperation.

## Research and Innovation: A National Priority

Research and innovation are here considered as searches for solutions to current global problems, such as the state of the environment and the consequences of climate change and the ageing and explosion of world populations. To this end, digital technologies and nanotechnologies are the great opportunities of the twenty-first century.[2]

It was for this purpose in 2009 that a national strategy for research and innovation was devised, which Valérie Pécresse, Minister of Higher Education and Research, described thus:

This is first a strategy based on the analysis of the great challenges to come, which constitute as many priorities for French research; it

---

[1] Ministère de l'Enseignement supérieur et de la Recherche [Ministry of Higher Education and Research], *Stratégie nationale de recherche et d'innovation, Rapport général, 2009* <http://media.enseignementsup-recherche.gouv.fr/file/SNRI/69/8/Rapport_general_de_la_SNRI_-_version_finale_65698.pdf>.

[2] <http://www.diplomatie.gouv.fr/fr/politique-etrangere-de-la-France/diplomatie-scientifique/article/document-de-strategie-une>.

is a truly national strategy: its priorities will therefore be defined in terms of the vital needs of the nation, to reassert the social value of research and innovation, and to revive the dialogue between science and society; it is primarily research-oriented: its priorities then have a place in the scheduling of research organizations, which will endow it with drive; it must power a transformation of research into innovation, by strengthening the interactive continuum between research and the needs of the market and of society, to lend a permanent dynamic between fundamental discoveries and their technological application, as well as their dissemination within our universities and *grandes écoles*.[3]

The three French priorities of research and innovation are

- health, wellbeing, food and biotechnology;

- the environment and ecological technologies; and

- information and communication technology and nanotechnologies

The demands of society for research into health are growing, and health, wellbeing, food and biotechnology offer many opportunities for economic development to French industry – in the pharmaceutical sector and in new health technologies. This research is of the first priority, organized around established goals: to research living organisms, from the genome to the ecosystem, to advance knowledge of its complexity, in particular by following cohorts of the population over time (a long-term observation of certain individuals, better to understand public health issues and developing models of living organisms by means of trials of simulation and prediction).

The more important public health issues are stressed: understanding and devising therapies for neurodegenerative illnesses, Alzheimer's disease in particular; studying the causes of infectious diseases, new or re-emerging, and developing the appropriate medicines; developing methods to restore the autonomy of dependent persons, the aged and the disabled, often with technological solutions, such as robotics, telemedicine and telehealth; preventing disease by encouraging better nutrition and increasing the traceability of food to ensure its security. Food also bears upon other elements of wellbeing: respect for the environment, organoleptic aspects and cultural identity.

[3] Ibid. (Preface).

An effort should be made to build strong bridges to create medical applications arising from fundamental research. This is the role of translational research: to establish efficient and sustainable links between academic researchers and those in industry with clinical researchers. Also important are the developing of key technologies for more personalized medicine and less invasive medical treatments – costing less but of comparable quality, such as rapid diagnosis, medical imaging and telemedicine – and the creation of a 'biotech plan' to boost the growth of biotechnology and synthetic biology companies.

Urgent action on the environment and environmental technologies are the second priority. As the effects of man's activities on the earth's equilibrium become apparent, there is an urgency to innovate to offer more sustainable development. In meeting this challenge, the opportunities for growth for French industry are considerable, making environmental technologies a national priority. This means a drive to understand and better model the evolution of climate change and of biodiversity, notably with effective means of measurement, often by satellite, and of simulation using supercomputers; to understand how living organisms react to external aggression, considering both toxicology and that of the environment, linked to human activities, and work towards better protection; to develop environmental technologies and concepts to make competitive products and provide services with minimal or zero environmental impact throughout their life cycles.

Ensuring a carbon-free energy future requires a balance between research on nuclear and renewable energies so as to preserve the environment: to identify the future technologies for nuclear energy in a logical framework of sustainable development (fourth-generation reactors, the nuclear fuel cycle and the management of radioactive waste); to improve the efficiency of existing photovoltaic cells and develop the future disruptive innovations, micro-layer technology and using organic materials; to value the whole planet, not simply its consumable parts, with new production processes using biofuels to avoid damaging competition in the uses of agricultural land; and to develop marine technologies: wave energy, tides and currents, thermal energy from the seas and offshore wind farms to exploit the exceptional maritime potential of France.

For sustainable town planning and transport, services and technologies require research: to improve the efficiency of motor vehicles and prepare the transition towards low $CO_2$ emissions and better – such as electric and hybrid vehicles; to reduce greenhouses gases and sound pollution from air transport by developing more efficient aircraft and optimizing the management of airspace; to devise sustainable models for buildings and cities by rethinking architecture and town planning and developing energy-stocking technologies.

The third priority addresses information and communication technology (ICT) and nanotechnologies. While ICT has generated a third industrial revolution which has transformed our everyday life, some are already ushering in fourth industrial revolution with the arrival of nanotechnologies in so many manufactured goods. French industry is poised to make a success of these upheavals, which are also major opportunities in the fight against exclusion and the development of carbon-free technologies. To ensure security and freedom for all, the uses to which these technologies are put must be the subject of research and sensible regulation.

The main challenges are:

- developing new technical alternatives for the Internet of the future or an internet of objects, in order to shape international standards, essential for the competitiveness of French industry;

- developing efficient computer architectures completely integrating hardware and software aspects to improve functionality, availability and reliability;

- strengthening the competitiveness of France's service industries such as banking, the media, school education and continuing education as well as high-tech manufacturing, including the motor car and aeronautical industries, with the capacity for software efficiency;

- maintaining France's leading position in the whole chain of software production (security is a major social and economic challenge, especially for virtual transactions and mobile adaptations of digital technologies); and

- making a success of the nanotechnology revolution in electronics, materials and health technologies, as well as renewable energies.

Ranking twentieth country by population, France is considered to be the fifth scientific power[4] and numbers some 220,000 state and private

---

[4] Ghislaine Filliatreau (ed.), *Indicateurs de sciences et de technologies: rapport de l'observatoire national des sciences et des techniques* (Paris: Economica, 2010).

researchers with over 800,000 engineers and scientists. With roughly 2 per cent of its gross domestic product devoted to research, France has scientific centres of world renown. These include mathematics, physics, nuclear science, space exploration, agronomy and archaeology. However, the French share of European industry has been declining for the last ten years, owing to a lack of investment in research and innovation. In fact, France has not sufficiently specialized in the scientific and technological domains that underlie the emerging sectors associated with bio- and nanotechnologies. Innovation consists of combining scientific abilities with bringing the results to the market, and France has not yet been able to achieve this sufficiently in order to be a player through international competition. In 2007, France ranked fifth in the world in the European system of patents (dropping one place compared with 2006):[5] thus, in both areas, France's share is diminishing in areas such as machinery, mechanics and transport in Europe, and pharmacy, biotechnology, chemistry and materials worldwide.

Space, a field where France and Europe excel, deserves special mention. After security and defence, the environment, telecommunications and satellites are significant applications for research and innovation in this sector. Space research trickles down to so many scientific and industrial applications: satellites and space probes are powerful observation tools for earth sciences and in order to study the universe, as well as for physics. The ambitious space programme stems from intergovernmental cooperation (European Space Agency) and European Union programmes, such as Galileo for navigation and the Global Monitoring for Environment and Security (GMES) for the observation of the earth.

French research and innovation have many strengths. As stated above, France is the fifth world power for science and technology – and in key and targeted research – with a major role in international scientific programmes and research for development. Significant state support (notably through research tax credits), sectors of excellence backed by powerful research organizations and a very highly qualified academic community, world leaders in transport and aeronautics, energy, services to the environment and food and agriculture, all give a steer to French research and innovation.

However, the weaknesses are a less visible and insufficiently coordinated

---

[5] In the American system, France also lost one place in 2007. The figures are those available in 2010.

system of research and higher education; an uncertain relationship between state research organizations, universities and business; insufficient private-sector investment in research and innovation and a reduced presence in developing sectors; somewhat limited partnerships with the emerging markets of Asia; and probably an over-rigid management of human resources in state institutions, which impacts career attractiveness, researcher mobility and the hosting of foreign researchers.

Since 2005, the French system of research and innovation has undergone significant reform, with the establishment of competitiveness centres,[6] the creation of the *Agence nationale de la recherche*[7] and of the *Agence d'évaluation de la recherche et de l'enseignement supérieur (Aeres)*,[8] a strengthening of university autonomy and support for public–private partnerships, notably through tax credits[9] and the *Instituts Carnots*.[10]

Two founding bills were passed by Parliament in 2006 and 2007 aimed at improving a complex system. The research bill of 18 April 2006 translates into law the '*Pacte pour la recherche*' between the citizens and the state; the bill of 10 August 2007 on the liberty and responsibilities of the universities strengthens their ability to take the initiative and seeks to improve their visibility both in Europe and more internationally.

## The *Equipements d'excellence* Project

On 20 January 2011, Valérie Pécresse, Minister of Higher Education and Research, and René Ricol, Commissioner-General for Investment, unveiled the fifty-two laureate projects representing the first round of calls for *Equipements d'excellence* projects.[11] With a total budget of €1 billion,

---

[6]   See <http://competitivite.gouv.fr>.

[7]   See <http://agence-nationale-recherche.fr>.

[8]   See <www.aeres-evaluation.fr>.

[9]   This fiscal measure, introduced in 1983, aims at mitigating research and development costs to companies through a tax reduction calculated as a function of their expenses here. In 2008, this measure was considerably strengthened and simplified and the upper limits relaxed.

[10]   This network comprises 13,000 researchers, with the main goal of facilitating technology transfers, partnerships between public laboratories and companies and developing innovation.

[11]   Source: <http://enseignementsup-recherche.gouv.fr/cid54722/340-millions-d-euros-pour-les-52-laureats-de-la-premiere-vague-de-l-appel-a-projets-equipex.html>.

this call for projects will enable French laboratories to access the latest scientific equipment in order to conduct world-class research programmes and increase knowledge and innovation.

At the end of this first round, €340 million will be allocated to the laureates: €260 million immediately for the purchase of the necessary equipment and €80 million paid to the beneficiaries of the projects over ten years to ensure the long-term financing of research equipment and associated maintenance and functioning costs.

The whole spectrum of research is represented in the fifty-two projects retained: 10 per cent in computer sciences, 10 per cent in the social sciences and humanities, 15 per cent in environmental sciences, 17 per cent for energy, 19 per cent for nanotechnologies and the remaining 29 per cent for biology and health.

- Mathematical modelling, which requires ever more powerful computers, includes the Equip@meso project, as, significantly, it will permit the setting up of a computer network to form a regional infrastructure of high performance.

- The social sciences and humanities, which require libraries and digital data banks, are represented by the Dime-SHS platform for the collecting and distribution of social data.

- In physics, the Rock project will permit the development of new materials, while the Socrates programme will look for new ways of harnessing solar energy.

- Environmental sciences, with projects such as the Integrated Arctic Ocean Observing System (iAOOS), aim at better understanding climate change by measuring parameters of the oceans and of the atmosphere;

- Health sciences, with a projects such as the IVTV research the ageing of cells, and Figures, which aims at developing innovative methods for facial surgery.

- Information and communication sciences are represented by project FD-SOI11, aimed at conceiving a new generation of electronic components.

It is the wish of Pécresse and Ricol that the allocation of these funds will have a leveraging effect and will attract co-funding from local authorities and private partners.

## Guiding Principles of the National Strategy for Research and Innovation

Fundamental research, a political choice, appears in the strengthening of the *Blanc* programme[12] of the *Agence nationale de la recherche* and the support France gives to the European Research Council. The autonomy of the universities, the setting up of ten new Institutes at the *Centre national de la recherche scientifique* (CNRS) within the framework of the performance contract signed with the state for 2009–13,[13] are designed to stimulate and develop the scientific communities.

Open research on society and the economy is linked to growth and employment. This competitiveness means that France must rebuild the links between state research institutions and business. For example, the tripling of tax credits for research enhances the fiscal attractiveness of France; indeed, this is a means to counteract offshoring and is thus a determining factor for growth and employment.

Better appreciation of risk and the need for security are implied in the combined challenges to the global community, such as climate change, the securing of energy supplies and the challenge of feeding the whole population of the world. These essential questions of risk and security must be tackled jointly with programmes of international cooperation.

In this context, the place of social sciences and the humanities, as well as a multidisciplinary approach, must be considered to permit a dialogue between the disciplines and an examination of how science and society are related.

## The Main Innovative Projects at the International Level

The seventh Framework Programme for Research and Development (FPRD) of the European Union is the essential funding tool for research

---

[12] This programme concerns all areas of research and aims at providing a strong support to original and ambitious projects in terms of international competition.

[13] *Institut des sciences biologiques* (INSB), *Institut de chimie* (INC), *Institut écologie et environnement* (INEE), *Institut des sciences humaines* (INSH), *Institut des sciences informatiques et de leurs interactions* (INS2I), *Institut des sciences de l'ingénierie et des systèmes* (Insis), *Institut national des sciences mathématiques et de leurs interactions* (Insmi), *Institut de physique* (INP), *Institut national de physique nucléaire et de physique des particules* (IN2P3) and *Institut national des sciences de l'univers* (Insu).

and innovation projects in Europe: for 2007–13, the 'Cooperation' strand will receive €32.4 billion.[14] This includes health, food, agriculture, fisheries and biotechnologies, information and communication technologies, nanosciences, nanotechnologies, materials and new production technologies, energy, the environment (including climate change), transport (including aviation), socioeconomic sciences and humanities, space, and security.

Collaborative research is the main object of this funding by the European Union, so as to establish research networks and projects capable of attracting researchers and investment from Europe and the wider world. There are two main thrusts: the Era-Net mechanism (European Research Area Network),[15] and the participation of the European Community in joint national research projects.[16]

Joint-technology initiatives concern long-term public–private partnerships in research and development in innovative medicine and pharmacy, embedded computing systems, aeronautics and aviation, projects in nanoelectronics, fuels and hydrogen, and other topics of a particularly strategic nature.[17]

The European technology platforms specify the fields of research and industry in the value-added European sectors: the restructuring of traditional industrial sectors such as steel and textiles, as well as space, embedded systems, aeronautics, mobile and wireless telecommunications, innovative medicine, transport, chemistry and natural resources, photovoltaic cells, water, biotechnologies, health and nano-medecine.[18]

The Competitiveness and Innovation Framework Programme is endowed with €3.6 billion for the period 2007–13 and addresses three main priorities: innovation and entrepreneurship, strategic support to information and communication technology and intelligent energy for Europe.[19]

---

[14] See <http://cordis.europa.eu/fp7/home_en.html>.

[15] A network of European public fundholders calling for proposals to finance collaborative projects in research, development and innovation. See <http://cordis.europa.eu/fp7/coordination/about-era_en.html>.

[16] Article 185 of the Lisbon Treaty. See <http://cordis.europa.eu/fp7/art185/home_en.html>.

[17] See <http://cordis.europa.eu/fp7/jtis/home_en.html>.

[18] See <http://cordis.europa.eu/technology-platforms/home_en.html>.

[19] Mainly aimed at small and medium-sized enterprises, this programme supports innovation (notably eco-innovation), improves access to finance and provides management services to businesses in the regions.

Also of importance are the European structural funds: the European Regional Development Fund (ERDF) and the European Social Fund (ESF), which finance a wide range of activities, from clusters[20] to infrastructures, from training to entrepreneurship, among many other intergovernmental programmes.

Proposals for the eighth Research and Technology Development Framework Programme (R&TDFP) and the European Research Area were the object of recommendations by the *Conférence des présidents d'universités* (CPU) [Conference of University Presidents], which were adopted unanimously at its plenary session on 20 January 2011.[21] These were the importance of European programmes integrating bottom-up and top-down approaches, the participation of universities in the implementation of this strategy, the need for simplification and harmonization, the importance of the triangle of knowledge – research, innovation, education – for universities, the expression of cooperation with joint programmes and the role of the regions.

### French International Expertise

France has taken measure of the financial challenge of the vast market in international expertise and the influence that can provide.[22] Many players – ministries and participants, regional and local authorities, parliament, private consultancy bureaus, business, academics, researchers and the whole of civil society – are involved in the promotion of international expertise in an approach that needs to be collective and methodical.

Expertise is primarily an essential component of the policies of solidarity with developing countries, particularly during and following periods of

[20] A grouping of research companies and higher education organizations in the same area of research forming a loose network.

[21] See <www.cpu.fr>.

[22] This section will study the main elements of a presentation made by Pierre Bühler during the July 2010 event organized by the Ministry of Foreign and European Affairs, 'Journées du réseau français dans le monde 2010'. Report to the prime minister by Nicolas Tenzer, 'L'expertise internationale au cœur de la diplomatie et de la coopération du XXIe siècle. Instruments pour une stratégie française de puissance et d'influence' (May 2008). Report by Jean Dussourd (prefect): 'Améliorer la gestion civilo-militaire des crises extérieures. Mettre en œuvre la stratégie interministérielle' (October 2009).

crisis. It is then a question of implementing the necessary operational expertise to reinstall the state in all its primary functions.

Expertise also is a means for the spread of social and legal norms and standards, as well as sanitation and environmental issues, from calls for tender in a huge market worth billions of dollars. Loans by the World Bank, European Union commitments and so-called 'vertical' funds, such as the global fund to fight Aids, tuberculosis and malaria, together with philanthropic foundations are complemented by bilateral arrangements and the activities of the emerging markets.

The key opportunities for French international expertise are in human resources – the link between training and the technical expertise service, facilitating dialogue between the diplomatic network and French experts, the market and that network, public–private partnerships, strategies of influence with international organizations and geographic priorities.

In the absence of a common definition of (and a recognizable qualification for) an 'expert', any contract for expertise agrees the modus operandi of an activity. So, the *Centre de coopération internationale en recherche agronomique pour le développement* (*Cirad*) has developed a 'guide to good practice' for its experts, and in early 2010 the Ministry for Higher Education and Research introduced a 'charter of expertise'. The contract of expertise is then tripartite between the organization that authorizes the service, that which receives it and the expert proper. This process allows the formalization in contract of essential areas such as, for example, an obligation to confidentiality, conflicts of interest and intellectual and industrial property rights. There still remains the difficult question of measuring international expertise in terms of a professional career, in the present context of the *Révision générale des politiques publiques* (RGPP) (the French general review of public policies) and the cutting or non-replacement of public posts. Finally, language skills and cultural preparation for 'experts' are essential elements in the preparation of expertise assignments.

The training of experts and of the trainers themselves is also a factor in the promotion of expertise, allowing the formation of a body of 'resource persons' who would act as agents of influence for development in each relevant sector.

Given the considerable number of operators, the diplomatic network can play an essential role in mobilizing French expertise by maintaining an alert for requests for expertise and passing them on, considering

French political interests in responding to calls for tender, identifying local partners and providing them with local and French contacts and extending diplomatic support to locally based players. The *Ubifrance* network[23] and that of the chambers of commerce and industry complement international funding agencies such as the European Commission and the World Bank. Market analysis and the French diplomatic network are agents for the expansion of expertise: thus, the extensive network of the *Instituts de recherche pour le développement* (IRDs) enables a better response to calls for expertise by being more intimately involved with the specific needs of prospective partners; similarly, the *Instituts Pasteur* network radiates French scientific influence very effectively. In addition to these vital networks are the philanthropic foundations, French regional and local authorities and non-governmental organizations.

For projects demanding expertise, public–private partnership is often the key to success: all the more so where the logistics of co-funding are vital to the progress of significant and high-budget projects. Thus, for transport, infrastructure projects, civil nuclear programmes and social and health initiatives, the support of the private sector complements that of the public sector.

Pierre Bühler outlines the main geographic target areas and the particular needs of each.[24]

- The emerging countries, notably Brazil, Russia, India and China, and the Gulf countries are increasingly sponsors of expertise in sustainable development, health and social protection, urban development, energy and the environment, higher education and research and culture.

- Eastern European and Mediterranean countries benefit from funding by the European Union within the framework of pre-accession and neighbourhood policies – mainly governance, infrastructure and agriculture.

- Multilateral sources of finance such as the World Bank, the European Union and the United Nations, and major foundations such as that of Bill and Melinda Gates, are the principal sponsors of expertise services to restore state functions in crisis-torn countries especially where the urgency of reconstruction is a pressing issue.

---

[23]  See <www.ubifrance.fr>.
[24]  See footnote 21, above.

- The French government also contributes aid to sub-Saharan Africa and French-speaking countries as preferred partners for the Ministry of Foreign and European Affairs, the technical ministries and state bodies.[25]

The parliamentary bill on the foreign activities of the French state, adopted on 12 July 2010, provides that 'the government will submit, at the latest one year after the promulgation of the present bill, a report proposing a strengthening of the cohesiveness of the state promotion of international technical expertise'.[26] These recommendations concern the articles of governance: the *Comité interministériel de la coopération internationale et du développement* (*Cicid*), the *Conseil d'orientation relatif au développement de l'expertise technique publique et privée*, the information and availability of human resources, the *Direction générale de la mondialisation, du développement et des partenariats* (DGM) and the role of *France Coopération/Expertise internationale*.

### Scientific Cooperation: A Prime Asset for Research and Partnership

Scientific cooperation is an essential sphere of French influence. This is due as much to the quality of the partnerships it creates as to the resulting networks which develop; it is often advanced with the cooperation of the universities, thus associating education with research.

At issue is the maintenance of a French presence among international networks of researchers and that of foreign researchers in France. Its main remit is 'to support the competitiveness of French and European research on the international scene and to back development research'[27] by paying particular attention to the research conducted with the developing countries of the South. Strengthening partnerships with industrialized countries in the sectors of research and innovation is also seen as important, as is the development of high-level scientific programmes with the major emerging markets.

[25] <http://www.diplomatie.gouv.fr/fr/politique-etrangere-de-la-france/aide-au-developpement-et/dispositifs-et-enjeux-de-l-aide-au/l-aide-publique-au-developpement/>.

[26] Title 1, Ch. IV, Art. 13.

[27] See <http://web.archive.org/web/20101204115633/http://www.diplomatie.gouv.fr/fr/actions-france_830/echanges-scientifiques-recherche_20149/index.html>.

Each diplomatic mission develops a specific policy on scientific cooperation, usually structured around vigilance in science and technology: following up on research and innovation policies and on the science and technology programmes in the host country, and taking charge of the dissemination of this information to the relevant institutions and organizations in France, also the promotion of bilateral and multilateral cooperation in science and technology and the awareness of French science and technology achievements in the country concerned.

Beyond these specific tasks targeting innovation, science and research, exchanges are organized around bilateral scientific programmes, such as the *Partenariats Hubert Curien* (PHC) [Hubert-Curien partnerships].[28] They can also be regional science partnerships able to develop existing research networks and create new ones in a given geographical area, as well as cooperation jointly funded with the regions within the framework of interdisciplinary programmes.

The sixty-seven Hubert-Curien partnerships and similar programmes are implemented by France and its partners and use a specific name according to country: scientific excellence, young researchers and innovative research are the main criteria for the calls for projects. Related programmes implemented in various countries and which proceed on the same scientific basis include the *Cofecub* (*Comité français d'évaluation de la coopération universitaire et scientifique avec le Brésil*) and the *Ecos* (*Évaluation et orientation de la coopération scientifique*) with Argentina, Chile, Colombia, Mexico, Uruguay and Venezuela.

Network research programmes (P2R) are themed mainly on health, water and the environment and are concerned with the development of research networks in China, Germany, India, Israel and South Africa.

One final example of a bilateral initiative are the *Frontières* programmes, launched in partnership with the Ministry of Higher Education and Research. The *Frontières de la science* and *Frontières de l'ingénierie* [engineering] programmes were launched in 2007 and 2010 to organize interdisciplinary seminars open to young researchers and representatives of bilateral collaboration.

There is a multitude of regional scientific partnerships active in establishing structured and lasting cooperation in the sciences: the *Bio-Asia* programme for the development of cooperation in the life

[28]  See <www.egide.asso.fr/jahia/Jahia/accueil/appels/phc/general>.

sciences in the ten countries of Asean[29] – the association of nations of South-East Asia, and others of the Far East and southern Asia; the *Stic-Asie* programme of collaboration in science and information and communication technologies; and the regional programme for mathematics and the life sciences in South America.

The *Arcus* programme, *Action en région de coopération universitaire et scientifique*, aims to bring the French regions to world attention.

In the social sciences and the humanities, France relies heavily on the network of twenty-seven research institutes abroad, under the joint responsibility of the Ministry of European and Foreign Affairs and the *Centre national de la recherche scientifique* and known as *Umifre – Unités mixtes-institut de recherche à l'étranger*; also significant are the 160 archaeological missions and the French archaeology schools abroad.

The role of French research institutes abroad is vital: a network of twenty-seven establishments with financial autonomy, extending to thirty-seven cities around the world, including branch offices.[30]

## The 'Maison Française d'Oxford'

Founded just after the Second World War by the universities of Paris and Oxford in the spirit of cooperation between the Allies who had just conquered totalitarianism, the Maison Française d'Oxford (MFO) has evolved into an interdisciplinary research laboratory in the field of social sciences and humanities.[31] Its partners, other than the two founding universities, are the French Ministry of Foreign and European Affairs and the *Institut des sciences humaines et sociales* of the CNRS. The MFO is one in the network of *Instituts français de recherche à l'étranger (Ifre)* – French research institutes abroad. It hosts a service and research unit of the CNRS to which eight researchers or researcher-teachers and one managerial

---

[29] Brunei, Cambodia, Indonesia, Laos, Malaysia, Myanmar, the Philippines, Singapore, Thailand and Vietnam.

[30] See <www.ifre.fr>.

[31] This passage on the Maison Française d'Oxford, written by its present Director Luc Borot, is taken from Maurice Fraser and Philippe Lane (eds), *Franco-British Academic Partnerships: The Next Chapter* (Liverpool University Press, 2011). See also Philippe Lane and Michael Worton (eds), *French Studies in and for the 21st Century* (Liverpool University Press, 2011).

agent are assigned. Seven others run the library and manage and maintain the two buildings which house eighteen postgraduate students active between master's and postdoctoral levels.

The MFO is a multidisciplinary centre undertaking comparative research in all its research projects, such as antiquities, literature, the history of science and political science. The main area of interest is Europe in the broader sense, but some programmes also concern Africa and Asia specialists.

The grounding of the MFO in the institutional fabric of the University of Oxford is exemplary in many respects: far from being on the fringes of the university and its colleges, institutes and faculties, its researchers and students are attached to the various components of the university, and the scientific events they organize are staged in close collaboration with British colleagues, who often initiate these proceedings.

The conventions signed with the constituent entities of the University of Oxford include co-financing and scientific cooperation together with exchanges of information on research programmes, to the benefit of French laboratories, universities and *grandes écoles* in France. The MFO is also a partner in several projects of the French national agency for research (ANR) and the European Science Foundation (ESF) along with British partners and collaborators from other European countries.

In this respect, the dialogue between the University of Oxford and the French embassy's university cooperation service and scientific service is warmly appreciated by the Oxford community. It is of note that the presence of the MFO encourages this coming together to the benefit of both countries to enrich the European and interdisciplinary dimensions of research in the social sciences at Oxford with British colleagues, by this French presence in their midst. The fact that academics outside Oxford (London for law, Birmingham for history, Leeds in political sciences) call upon the MFO to mount collaborative projects on France with their colleagues from Oxford and from France bears witness to the place of the MFO among British universities as a respected working institution, a hub for inter-university collaboration.

## University Cooperation: On the Boundaries of Higher Education, General Education and Culture

University cooperation brings about numerous cultural and scientific exchanges. Whilst it is closely involved in educational and cultural projects, it is also an essential component of science and technology. It is the target of the law relative to the freedom and responsibilities of universities, brought in by Valérie Pécresse, Minister of Higher Education and Research on 10 August 2007.[32]

University cooperation relies mainly on four complementary approaches: training and research networks, student and teacher exchanges, the exchange of good practice and the university subject of French studies.

Networking certainly is an important part of university cooperation. The creation in 2005 of the *Agence nationale de la recherche*, after the model of research funding organizations in other countries and at the European level (European Research Council), encourages the creation of new networks. These often rely on double degrees (notably master's degrees) or joint degrees (co-directing or co-tutoring of theses). The creation of chairs of visiting professor also proved an effective means of developing and strengthening these networks: such invitations constitute a desirable means of initiating strong and lasting relations between universities and of bringing French research to a wider audience. Double degrees and joint degrees often originate in these partnerships or are a part of European (*Erasmus* or *Erasmus Mundus*) or bilateral programmes: they concern universities, *grandes écoles* and specialized institutions. If bachelor and master's degrees are well-understood levels of study in this labelling process, the doctorate level is often more difficult to implement in a regime of co-tutoring, since regulatory measures and costs can be very different from one country to another. University and scientific cooperation services must then play their full role in liaising between the universities and the administrations concerned.

Student exchange and the promotion of French higher education form a considerable part of university cooperation: significant here is the

---

[32] See also Cécile Hoareau, 'Globalization and Dual Modes of Higher Education Policy-making in France: *je t'aime moi non plus*', Center for Studies in Higher Education (CSHE), Research and Occasional Paper Series, 2.11 (January 2001) <http://cshe.berkeley.edu/publications/publications.php?id=376>.

work of the *CampusFrance* agency,[33] which complements that of *Egide*.[34] Attracting high-flying international exchange students to France together with the internationalization of higher education establishments in the context of a renewed French academic scene are specific goals for greater international influence. The availability of places for exchange students, the attractiveness of France, the offer of a university education, promotion events and the international networks and programmes tend to put French higher education establishments foremost at an international level. An important element strengthening the attractiveness of French higher education is that some courses are conducted through the medium of English in French universities, as is already the case in some of the *grandes écoles* and other specialized institutions (similar to provision in the Netherlands, which offers over 1,000 university courses in the English language in very diverse sectors). Of note for student exchanges are the grant programmes[35] and the role played by student associations. Of significance is the work of the *CampusFrance* agency, which includes that of *Egide* and, for international activities, the *Centre national des œuvres universitaires et scolaires* (*Cnous*).

## Student Mobility in the World: Some Key Figures

In 2008, 2,893,280 students in France benefited from exchanges around the world, up by 24 per cent since 2003.[36] Most came from Asia, followed by Europe and Africa – Chinese, then Indian, South Korean, German and Japanese students being the most active. In the same year, the countries receiving most international students were the United States (624,474), the United Kingdom (341,791), France (243,436), Australia (230,635) and Germany (189,347). Chinese students formed the largest group in the United States, the United Kingdom, Australia and Germany. In 2007–8, incoming exchange students to France, at 263,939, totalled some four

---

[33] See <www.campusfrance.org/en>.

[34] See <www.egide.fr>.

[35] The grant programmes are at different levels – bachelor, master's and doctorate – such as international doctoral exchanges: *Les notes de Campus-France*, 28 (February 2011) <www.campusfrance.org>.

[36] Source: Les étudiants internationaux: chiffres clés CampusFrance 2010 <http://www.campusfrance.org/en/node/4220>.

times the number of French students going abroad to study (67,606). Of these, only Morocco sent more students to France than did China. France is the second country for *Erasmus* students, both inward and outward: 20,053 in 2007–8. Only Spain exceeded this number (with 27,831 students).

Exchanges of good practice allow for the detailed monitoring of the evolution of higher education and research around the world, as well as the evaluation and funding of research. At a time of university reform, it is essential that the various issues of higher education are addressed: funding (including tuition costs), evaluation, internationalization and the exchange of students, the brain drain (and remedial programmes), university governance and university relations with business. A very sensitive issue is international ranking: figures are published regularly in the international press, to the great dismay of some countries, including France. The rankings of Jiao-Tong university in Shanghai and the (UK) *Times Higher Education* rely on such criteria as publishing, university size and the number of students, which do not necessarily favour French universities. It will be of particular interest to observe the progress of the proposed European ranking project for higher education establishments.

The prevalance of the French language[37] and of French studies around the world is a unique network of influence and dissemination for French scientific and cultural diplomacy, reaching out to the 220 million French speakers in the world.[38] Five major programmes define the efforts of the *Agence universitaire de la francophonie* (AUF):

- the French language and cultural and linguistic diversity;

- aspects of democracy and the rule of law;

- reinforcement of academic excellence, partnerships and relations with business;

- innovation through information and communication technology for education; and

- and the environment and sustainable and fair development.

---

[37] See <www.auf.org>.

[38] French is the official language of twenty-seven states and three governments.

With its nine regional offices and its presence on the Internet and television (TV 5Monde), the AUF is a major force in the promotion of the French language and international development, since linguistic and cultural interests are intertwined with the political desire for development of the countries where the agency undertakes its areas of cooperation. The training of executive staff and leaders has also become an issue for the French-speaking world, as Bernard Cerquiglini so aptly stressed about the training of a francophone elite.[39]

To conclude, French studies, such as is represented by French associations, study societies and international conferences, touches upon very diverse subjects and is an ideal platform for the exchange of ideas on contemporary issues (such as literature, linguistics, women's and feminist studies, cinematographic studies and post-colonial studies). University cooperation often relies on these networks of French studies, which are a way into the faculties and laboratories of universities where they flourish.

## The Budget of the *Agence universitaire de la francophonie* (AUF)

In 2008, the initial budget of the AUF was €40 million, financed by France up to 79 per cent at €30.9 million, Canada with €2.5 million, Quebec €1.2 million, the Belgian French community €0.5 million and Switzerland €0.09 million. Programme expenditure represents 79.6 per cent of the agency's budget (€31.3 million) against 3.2 per cent for institutional expenses and 16.6 per cent for administrative expenses.

The 2008 budget, the third in the four-year plan of the agency, emphasizes action in support of academic excellence (see Table 5.1).

[39] Bernard Ciquiglini, 'La formation des élites francophones', *Géoéconomie*, 55 (autumn 2010), pp. 99–105.

Table 5.1 *Breakdown of expenses between the five programmes defining the efforts of the Agence universitaire de la francophonie, 2006–2008 (€ million)*

|  | 2006 | 2007 | 2008 |
| --- | --- | --- | --- |
| The French language and cultural and linguistic diversity | 3.521 | 2.160 | 2.046 |
| Aspects of democracy and the rule of law | 0.721 | 0.787 | 0.724 |
| Reinforcement of academic excellence, partnerships and relations with business | 13.854 | 15.313 | 15.661 |
| Innovation through information and communication technology for education | 7.781 | 8.097 | 8.536 |
| The environment and sustainable and fair development | 6.377 | 4.643 | 4.381 |
| Others | – | – | 0.863 |
| Totals | 32.254 | 31.000 | 32.211 |

*Source*: www.auf.org.

# 6

# Linguistic and Educational Cooperation

## Linguistic Cooperation: A Multifaceted Agent of French Influence

French language policies form one of the foundations of French foreign cultural initiatives. The development of cultural and scientific exchanges goes hand in hand with the promotion of the French language, an essential component of the policy of influence around the world.

The *Observatoire de la langue française* of the *Organisation internationale de la francophonie* (OIF) publishes an annual report on the situation of French and its evolution in the world.[1] This report attempts to estimate the number of French speakers, the teaching of French through the medium of the French language, and the international dimension of the language. It benefits from contributions from the Ministry of Foreign and European Affairs, as well as the diplomatic and cultural network.[2] This study by the OIF includes member and observer countries – less than half use French as the official language – but also countries not in the OIF where the number of practising French speakers is significant, such as in Algeria, with 11.2 million, Israel, with about 500,000, and the United States, where 2.1 million speak French.

In total, over 220 million people can be defined as francophone – up by 10 per cent from 2007 – foremost in Europe, with 40 per cent of the total, followed by sub-Saharan Africa and the Indian Ocean, with 36 per

[1] Organisation internationale de la francophonie, *La langue française dans le monde 2010* (Paris: Nathan, 2010).

[2] Notably from Laurent Lapeyre and Jen-Paul Rebaud, of the *Direction générale de la mondialisation, du développement et des partenariats (sous-direction de la diversité linguistique et du français)* (2010).

cent, North Africa and the Middle East, with 15 per cent, the Americas and the Caribbean, with 8 per cent, with the remaining 1 per cent in Asia and Oceania.

The French language is the ninth most spoken language in the world, after Mandarin, Spanish, English, Hindi, Arabic, Portuguese, Russian and Bengali. The OIF considers this statistic to be somewhat understated, in that it does not take account of the people from other countries who can express themselves in French or can understand the language: the number of people who can speak or understand French occasionally or partially is likely to be around 300 million.

The original aim of this study concerned the teaching *of* and *in* French. If French is the language of schools and higher education in francophone countries (teaching *in* French), it is also one of the very few foreign languages taught (teaching *of* French) in almost all the countries of the world – second only to English. Present in school and university systems, it is also promoted and taught by bilateral and multilateral cooperation networks and essential in the role of the network of *Alliances françaises* all over the world. Thus, over 116 million people are learning French. Most of these are in sub-Saharan Africa and the Indian Ocean, with a figure of 44 per cent in 2010; next are learners in Europe, with 23.4 per cent; but also in north Africa and the Middle East, with 22.6 per cent; the Americas and the Caribbean, with 8 per cent; and Asia-Oceania with 2 per cent. Since 2007, these figures have grown by an average of 13 per cent. But this global progression conceals regional disparities: the rise in numbers is mainly on the African continent as a result of improvements in schooling in these countries, where French is the main language for teaching – up by 31 per cent. Sub-Saharan Africa, with 96.2 million French speakers, is where French speakers are most numerous, all of which is made clear in a report by Rocheboine and Schneider in 2007.[3] So, demographic pressures call for an improvement in French teaching before 2015. However, there is a continuing tendency for the number of people learning French in Europe to decrease – it is down by 17 per cent in the same period.

[3] François Rocheboine and André Schneider, 'Rapport d'information déposé en application de l'article 145 du règlement par la commission des affaires étrangères en conclusion d'une mission d'information constituée le 11 avril 2006 sur la situation de la langue française dans le monde', rapport d'information 3693 (Assemblée Nationale, Paris, 13 February 2007).

The international dimension of the French language can be judged from its presence in multilateral organizations and networks, most notably the Internet and broadcasting. If the domination of English is still a force in major international institutions, there has been some evolution noted since 2006 in the preparations for the Olympic Games. As we have seen above, in broadcasting, TV5 Monde is one of the five largest television networks in the world, with a global reach in the French language of some 210 million homes around the world, feeding around 6,000 cable networks in over 200 countries.

The role of operators in the French language is vital: the *Agence universitaire de la francophonie*,[4] the *Assemblée parlementaire de la francophonie*,[5] TV5 Monde, Sedar Senghor University in Alexandria[6] and the *Association internationale des maires francophones* all play a significant part – taken over in 2010 by the *Maison de la francophonie* in Paris.

Also active is the personal representative of the French president for the French language, Jean-Pierre Raffarin. Asserting the importance of multilingualism as an element of cultural diversity and of the French-speaking geographical area as a political space, the promotion of the French language within international organizations is a means of promoting multilingualism as a constituent of cultural diversity. This francophone claim carries with it the obligation for senior officials to speak French when this language is an official or working language. For this claim for French to be credible, the offer for French and training must be effectively developed. Similarly, use of French does not only concern questions of language or culture but also international topics, such as sustainable development and climate change.

Moreover, the full range of international institutions shows a rather diverse record with respect to multilingualism: financial constraints linked to translation, recruiting procedures, communications policies and a tendency to reluctance on the part of the French and francophone

---

[4] A global network of higher education and research establishments created in 1961 and comprising 774 establishments covering every continent, in 90 countries, 55 of which are members of the OIF.

[5] Founded in 1967, it is a place for debates, proposals and the exchange of information on all subjects of common interest to its members. It presently numbers 48 member sections, 17 associated parliaments and 12 observers.

[6] Founded in 1990, its official title is the *Université internationale de langue française au service du développement africain*.

players make it necessary to be increasingly watchful in the daily practice of multilingualism.

This highlights the importance of the *Semaine de la langue française* week and of the *Journée internationale de la francophonie* day every 20 March.[7] Thus, in 2010, over 2,500 events were organized around the French language in almost 200 diplomatic or consular missions to promote cultural diversity and linguistic exchange. It was also an occasion to celebrate the forty years of the *Organisation internationale de la franco-phonie.*

### *Semaine de la langue française et de la francophonie,* 13–20 March 2011: '*Dis-moi dix mots qui nous relient*'

This is a week for French and all things francophone – an occasion to celebrate the vitality of French language, the tool par excellence of social links, of personal expression, and of access to citizenship and culture.

On the initiative of the Ministry for Culture and Communication, the *Délégation générale à la langue française et aux langues de France* (DGLFLF), the week is organized each year around ten words and one theme. In 2011, the ten words chosen illustrated the bond of solidarity, which, through a shared language, links members of a community: 'welcoming, feast, with, choir, accomplice, roped together, thread, harmoniously, hand, networking'. Through French, it is a whole set of imaginations, values, gazes, singular projects set upon the world. This link between French speakers is all the more profound and fruitful in that it is enriched by different cultures, other identities and other languages. Creativity workshops, contests, debates of ideas, exhibitions, new technologies, performing arts and media events enabled exchange between French speakers, Francophiles and promoters of the French language.

In addition, the *Observatoire de l'espace* of the *Centre national d'études spatiales* (*Cnes*) organized a contest called '*L'espace en jeu*' [Space in play], based on a creation kit. And, for its part, the *Fédération internationale des professeurs de français* (FIPF) organized a blog contest on the theme of sharing and solidarity, in collaboration with the DGLFLF.

Respect for the French language and the renaissance of French

---

[7]   See <http://latitudefrance.org>.

speaking are at the heart of French foreign cultural policies. The 'weight of languages', an expression and an important research topic of Alain Calvet and Jean-Louis Calvet.[8] The space given in the media, the role of scientific communication, the presence on the Internet, international norms and French speaking, diplomatic documentation, cooperation with central administrations and permanent diplomatic posts are some of the many places and issues for the presence and development of French as a language.[9]

This linguistic action comes in a variety of forms, according to the geographic zone in which it takes place. Thus, in Europe, the emphasis is put on the use of French as a working language of the European Union, on the compulsory teaching of two foreign languages in national education systems, on the initial and continuing training of teachers of French and on the development of bilingual French teaching.

In North Africa and the Middle East, the situations are contrasted. In the Maghreb, the reintroduction of French to the school curriculum is accompanied by a programme of initial and in-service training for primary school teachers and for teachers of French at the secondary level. In the Near East, although the old tradition of French speaking is still alive, a new context of Arabic–English–French trilingualism clearly emerges to answer a perceived need for cultural and linguistic diversification. In the Gulf states, the call for French is by cultural establishments and universities, as alternatives, albeit limited, to an all-English offer.

Africa is without doubt the priority area of linguistic and education cooperation development, the two dimensions being closely aligned. Amongst the twenty-nine states to have adopted French as their official language, twenty-two are situated in sub-Saharan Africa. This choice accompanies development policies in three main areas:

- improving knowledge of French, the language of teaching and early learning, with the support of national education systems;

---

[8] See <http://web.archive.org/web/20120226180230/http://www.portalingua.info/fr/poids-des-langues>.

[9] See 'Rapport au Parlement sur l'emploi de la langue française', Délégation générale à la langue française et aux langues de France, Ministry of Culture and Communication, Paris, October 2010: foreword by Frédéric Mitterrand, Minister of Culture and Communication.

- favouring the use of French in daily social life, with the help of local media; and

- professionalizing the teaching of French, with the centres for French as a foreign language.

This proactive approach is complemented by training programmes for teachers undertaken with the education authorities of the countries concerned, most often within the *Fonds de solidarité prioritaire* (FSP) priority solidarity fund. It is a basis of partnerships with states, fund providers and those active in civil society. A distinction is made between 'country' projects, that is bilateral projects contributing to the development of a partner country, 'inter-state' projects benefiting a set group of countries, often united in an intergovernmental organization, and 'enabling programmes', which are contributions to sectoral development by theme. Mayotte and Reunion Island also offer strong anchoring points for linguistic cooperation.

In Asia, linguistic cooperation is an increasing factor in the teaching of French alongside other languages and concerns all levels of the education system. The present tendency favours the orienting of linguistic expertise towards science and technological culture. Many projects aimed at enhancing French are actually framed with an educational dimension which confers a more sustainable quality in the short or long terms. Special mention should be given to specific forms of cooperation with the major emerging countries (China, India and Indonesia), northern Asia (Hong Kong, Japan, Korea, Singapore and Taiwan) and to projects in South-East Asia (Cambodia, Laos, Thailand and Vietnam).

North America poses an altogether different approach to linguistic dissemination: the network of *Alliances françaises* and Institutes is an essential factor and university departments of French Studies also contribute to the high quality of provision in French. Of note are the active policies of Louisiana and Quebec, favouring the French language, bilingualism and multilingualism in their education systems.

Central and South America use four international languages: Spanish, Portuguese, French and English. Together with all the local languages, there is enormous linguistic diversity. This must be taken into account in all the language development programmes, including in the overseas *départements* of Guadeloupe, Guyane and Martinique. The French teachers' associations thus have a significant role in language-based cooperation programmes and constitute as many agents of educational action in the broadest sense.

Linguistic cooperation is extremely strong with Australia and New Zealand. This ties in with the southern Pacific, notably New Caledonia. These countries are good bases for wider regional cooperation, with the setting up of training and research initiatives.

The promotion of French is thus an essential part of linguistic cooperation. And not just the maintenance of the language, as shown by some specific applications: French as the language of schooling in Africa; French and development; French and sports; French as the language of education for foreign leaders of business and state. All these are conduits promoting the language.

In African francophone countries, French is the teaching language or the second language. It also has an important role in the education systems of countries where English, Arabic, Spanish or Portuguese is the dominant language. The *Agence française pour le développement* (AFD), the *Agence pour l'enseignement du français à l'étranger* (AEFE), the cultural establishments – centres, Institutes and *Alliances françaises* – all have an important role to play in cooperation and dissemination. The *Agence universitaire de la francophonie* and the *Organisation internationale de la francophonie* promote cooperation which goes well beyond the linguistic.

French is thus one of the languages providing access to economic and social development, beyond the strictly educational and scientific. Help for schooling, 'French as a second language' networks, policies in support of bilingualism – as in Madagascar – are most often linked to more ambitious programmes of development aid. This is also the case with support for French in the major African international organizations.

French plays a specialized role in sport: English and French are the official languages of the Olympic Movement. The use of French in sport deserves special attention. In the Vancouver Winter Games of 2010, bilingualism was fully respected: all official announcements were made in French and then in English, all commentaries during events had a significant place for French, displays were bilingual and many volunteers were French speakers.

Through the French language, France also participates in the education of foreign top professionals with its network of establishments abroad, through academic, scientific and technical training, and within the major international organizations. This last point is noteworthy, since it should ensure a generational permanence in linguistic cooperation.

### Educational Links: A Tool for Sustainable Cooperation

The three main thrusts for educational cooperation are:

- developing and strengthening the network of French bilingual teaching, with some 200,000 school students in the bilingual sections of fifty-three countries over five continents;

- providing teacher training, taking into account the rapid evolution of technologies and generational renewal; and

- responding more specifically to the needs generated by the status of French in Africa.

The French schools' network is unique in its numbers and its geographic ambit: it is run by the *Agence pour l'enseignement du français à l'étranger* (AEFE), a state administrative body directed by the Ministry for Foreign and European Affairs. The *Mission laïque française*, a partner of this ministry, aims at diffusing French language and culture through schools abroad.

Indeed, France possesses the foremost foreign school network of any country, present in 130 countries with some 461 *lycées*, and about 260,000 students. At the beginning of school year 2009–10, these numbers were up by almost 2,500. In 2009, some 12,000 students took their *baccalaureate* in the schools of the network: 94 per cent passed, 62 per cent with honours.

Development priorities more specifically concern evolution towards emerging countries, the involvement of the schools network in international education cooperation, promoting university cooperation and the search for new sources of funding such as public–private finance.

The recommendations made by Julia Kristeva-Joyaux in her report 'Le message culturel de la France et la vocation interculturelle de la francophonie'[10] have a particular emphasis on education, key to developing

---

[10]   Julia Kristeva-Joyaux, 'Le message culturel de la France et la vocation interculturelle de la francophonie'. Avis du Conseil économique, social et environnemental présenté par Julia Kristeva-Joyaux, rappporteur, au nom de la section des relations extérieures (Paris: CESE, 2009).

French influence and attractiveness. In this field, AEFE is an essential agent of a French policy of influence. Beyond the traditional role of public service relative to the education of French children abroad there is also a need to allocate school grants in order to strengthen cooperation in relations between France, the French language and foreign education systems. French language and culture are also influenced by the hosting of foreign students in France. During its 19 May 2010 session, the AEFE adopted a new strategic four-point plan for 2010–13.

First, to develop a teaching of excellence, responding to the demands and expectations of French and foreign students. This goal, assuring the essential aims of French teaching, depends on an army of permanent teachers. With the *baccalaureate* a central element, training gains in responding to other internationally recognized methods of certification, notably in modern languages. Collaborating with the *Cned* (the national centre for distance learning), the *Onisep* (the national office for information on trainings and professions), the *Scérén* (services, culture, publishing, resources for national education) (formerly the CNDP, national centre for pedagogical documentation) and TV5 Monde provides a significant training offer through a range of media.

Second, to accelerate the modernization of the network better to respond to the needs of families to further cultural influence. The AEFE has been assigned to the evaluation and increased professionalization of human resource management and to the autonomy and management of the establishments.

Third, to improve the running of the network. This has always been a sensitive issue because it concerns French foreign policy priorities and conditions in the local context or the level of language competition in the country concerned.

Fourth, to find a balance which guarantees the functioning and growth of the network. The issue is mainly to strike a financial balance which optimizes the schooling and education offer in the context of current state policies and which examines closely the establishment of new approved establishments. The Flam programme for the consolidation of French as mother tongue, founded in 2001–2, numbered some 4,500 young learners by 2009, 2,300 of whom were aged between 5 and 16. Some sixty-two associations were supported financially in some twenty countries.

## The French Education Network Abroad

In 2010, foreign centres of French education numbered 461 in more than 130 countries, each in one of three principal categories: officially recognized, registered or directly managed. The previous year, the network consisted of 452 establishments.[11]

The seventy-seven centres under direct control are external services of the AEFE, the agency for the teaching of French abroad; the 166 registered establishments are managed by associations subject to French or local business law that have signed an agreement with the AEFE, which includes the posting and remuneration of the permanent employees and subsidies and relations with the agency. Both categories of establishment receive subsidies from the agency, which also regulates the salaries for permanent employees, with the subsidy granted by the French government and the income to the establishments from tuition fees paid by benefiting families.

The 212 establishments which are simply registered, have not signed an agreement with the agency and receive no direct help. On request, however, they can be associated with continuing education initiatives organized by the AEFE and can benefit from counselling by the *inspecteurs de l'éducation nationale* abroad.

The AEFE encourages the development of the network by signing partnership agreements which allow for control that is flexible, diversified and as close as possible to the needs of each establishment. This hybrid status between recognized and registered concerns six establishments: the Lycée Franco-Israelien in Tel Aviv, the Lycée Théodore Monod in Abu Dhabi, the French section of the European School in Taipei, the French International School in Bali, the French School in Tashkent and the Interkulturelle Schule in Bremen.

Supervision by the embassies varies also, according to the nature of the establishment. Embassy staff work closely with the AEFE when decisions concern establishments under direct management. For establishments which are registered, the ambassador, or his or her counsellor for cooperation and cultural initiatives, is often an ex-officio governor.

The total number of French children in the schools network under

[11] Source: Geneviève Colot, 'Rapport d'information déposé en application de l'article 145 du règlement par la commission des affaires étrangères en conclusion des travaux d'une mission d'information constituée le 28 janvier 2009 sur "le rayonnement de la France par l'enseignement et la culture"' (Assemblée Nationale, Paris, January 2010).

direct management or registered has evolved from 78,640 students in 2007–8 to 82,221 in 2008–9. Non-French students numbered 89,332 in 2007–8 and 91,371 in 2008–9. This shows the network is still growing in number, both in terms of schools and of students.

This network is not rigid: every year sees start-ups, closures and changes in status. A recent example of an establishment joining the network is the *Centre d'appui à la réouverture des établissements d'enseignement français en Côte d'Ivoire* – the centre to support French education establishments in the Ivory Coast – formed on 1 September 2008 to facilitate the reopening of, amongst others, the Lycée Français Blaise Pascal in Abidjan for the school year 2008–9, with the status of registered establishment. That year it received 950 students, and 1,200 at the start of the following school year.

The network of the *Mission laïque française* supervises 107 education establishments in nearly forty countries, receiving some 40,000 students. Historically located in the Mediterranean countries, it has spread to the United States and the Gulf states. In conjunction with French companies located abroad and the education authorities of countries emerging from crisis, the *Mission laïque française* plays a key role in cooperation that complements its central activity of education, as outlined in its strategy document for 2010–12.

One of the main challenges for education cooperation for the years to come is the rapid growth of francophone bilingual teaching. Within such bilingual sections, teachers work in two languages: the local language and French. In this kind of teaching of French, the French language becomes the medium for learning one or more additional subjects, such as science or history. The objectives and programmes are defined by the local country's education authorities. The teachers are their nationals and can be assisted by practitioners seconded from France, and a specific certification accompanies the final evaluation.

The initial and continuing education of teachers is also an important part of cooperation and is led jointly by the *Centre international d'études pédagogiques* (*Ciep*) in Sèvres and the *Bureau pour l'enseignement de la langue et de la civilisation françaises à l'étranger* (*Belc*) (founded in 1959). Of concern are teaching methods for French as a first or second language, francophone bilingual teaching, training techniques for teachers of French as a second language, education methods and the training of those who are themselves involved in teacher training.

One particularly significant development for the teaching of science in schools is *La main à la pâte* (hands-on). Started in 1996 on the initiative of Nobel laureate in physics Georges Charpak, this programme aims at promoting a scientific investigative approach in primary schools. It is operated by the *Académie des sciences*, with support from the *Institut national de la recherche pédagogique* and the *École normale supérieure*, and it is based on an agreement between the French Ministries of Education and of Higher Education and Research.

The examination and certification of knowledge and ability in the French language affects the provision of training. The *Diplôme d'études en langue française* (*Delf*), the *Diplôme approfondi de langue française* (*Dalf*), the *Diplôme de français Professionnel* (DFP) – delivered by the *Chambre de commerce et d'industrie de Paris* (CCIP) – the *Diplômes d'université* (DUs), the *Test de connaissance du français* (TCF) and the *Test d'évaluation de français* (TEF) – conceived and delivered by the CCIP – provide a variety of ways to evaluate language abilities.

If general education is at the heart of education cooperation, there is also a role for professional and technical training, particularly with regard to development, to make up for the deficiencies in child schooling, the education deficit for girls and a stretched presence in rural areas. This would foster intermediate qualifications, mainly in the services sector. The certification of professional qualifications is a major area for development and partnerships with the countries concerned.

For teaching, education cooperation and professional training are the two fundamental elements of foreign aid programmes.

## French Aid for Education in Developing Countries, 2010–2015

French support for development is a major priority in the education sector,[12] one of the key elements of development. This is the choice of the countries with which France has partnerships: out of thirty-two framework documents for partnership, nineteen prioritize education and make the promotion of French as a world language a common factor of cooperation.

[12] Source: <http://web.archive.org/web/20110528233048/http://www.diplomatie.gouv.fr/fr/ministere_817/publications_827/enjeux-planetaires-cooperation-internationale_3030/documents-strategie-sectorielle_20004/action-exterieure-france-pour-education-dans-les-pays-developpement-2010-2015_80307.html>.

In promoting solidarity, everyone can exercise their rights by gaining access to knowledge, languages, expertise and ideas. It is a strategic choice for sustainable growth and the fight against poverty in all its guises, the demographic transition of developing countries and a factor of general health improvement.

On the basis of diagnostics and priorities shared with partner countries, this choice increases the effectiveness of French aid, much in the spirit of the Paris Declaration of 2005 and the Accra Agenda of 2008.[13]

Within this framework, France has decided to promote two major objectives by the year 2015: to provide a decisive contribution to universal primary schooling and to a parity of access to education for girls and boys; and to promote an integrated vision for education, including primary and secondary education, vocational training and higher education, so as better to respond to the future needs of youth in a new strategy covering the whole education sector.

The fulfilment of these objectives depends on a policy of promotion of French as a language giving access to knowledge, particularly in francophone Africa, where French is the teaching language. To achieve this, France is reviewing and improving the instruments and systems hitherto used and strengthening the capacities of the countries receiving help in maintaining their education systems.

In the developed world, linguistic and education cooperation link training, international institutions and the education system. Two initiatives need to be developed: innovative projects on the Internet, and international efforts in conjunction with business.

In emerging and developing countries, the expansion of francophone bilingual teaching, the training of teachers, economic and social progress and higher education are activities which encourage joint programmes of cooperation. Finally, the education element of research and development should support efforts to involve the developing countries of the South

---

[13] The Paris Declaration is an international agreement approved on 2 March 2005 by some 100 ministers, executives from aid organizations and other high-ranking officials, aiming at an increase, by the governments and organizations they represented, in efforts of harmonization, alignment and management to improve the results of aid to development, through activities allowing follow-up reports and the use of sets of indicators. It is the strongest commitment to development aid yet, in that it redefines the relations between donor and recipient countries. It was ratified by the adoption of an agenda in Accra, Ghana, in September 2008.

in scientific programmes and networks for research on the major global issues of our time.

Indeed, the linguistic and education dimension cannot be divorced from scientific and academic cooperation: if areas of partnership and challenges differ, there exists a continuum of research and activities of concern specific to geographic groups of developing countries in the South.

# 7

# The Organization and Implementation
# of French Cultural and Scientific Activities
# Abroad

The foreign cultural and scientific initiatives of France rely on a network of *Instituts français* and *Alliances françaises*, research centres and cultural centres, constituting, with all the French schools and *lycées* abroad, an unmatched network.

## A Global Network of Cultural and Science Cooperation

In this chapter, we shall restate and examine the annual French draft diplomatic programme for culture and influence abroad – Programmes 185 and 209. Christian Masset, *directeur général de la mondialisation, du développement et des partenariats*, has stated that 'reform of the network for cooperation initiated with the general review of public policies (RGPP) will be shaped over the years from 2011 to 2013'.[1] Thus 2011 is seen as a pivotal year, with the implementation of a comprehensive and ambitious reform of the foreign activities of the state.

This includes local mergers abroad of cultural centres and Institutes with the agents in the embassies of the *service de coopération et d'action culturelle* (*Scac*) –cooperation and cultural activities. In the ninety-four countries with an institution enjoying financial autonomy, there will be:

- one unified institution having financial autonomy and attached initially to the relevant embassy;

---

[1] See especially the general presentation by Christian Masset. <www.performance-publique.budget.gouv.fr/farandole/2011/pap/html/DBGPGMPRESSTRATPGM185.htm>.

- the creation of the *Institut français*, with expertise in artistic exchanges, ideas, language, culture and knowledge;

- a strengthening of the mutual benefits between the networks of *Alliances françaises* and the *Institut français*, regarding cultural activities and cooperation services; and

- the rationalization of financing, human resources and strategic control, conforming with geographic priorities.

The aspirations are to be realized through certain strategies and priorities. The *Institut français*, which replaced *CulturesFrance*, will be piloted from 2011 in Cambodia, Chile, Denmark, Georgia, Ghana, India, Kuwait, Senegal, Serbia, Singapore, Syria, the United Arab Emirates and the United Kingdom. The French language as a European and international language will be a training priority for students, researchers, senior officials and opinion leaders. The teaching of French abroad is the subject of new contracts with agreed objectives. The implementation of a policy of scientific and academic attractiveness will promote inward exchanges. There will be a search for new high-level scientific partnerships and exchanges of expertise, notably in the life sciences, nanotechnologies and multidisciplinary sciences. World public concerns, such as the environment, health, financial and economic stability, food security and the diffusion of knowledge are essential issues, supported specifically by Programme 209 for aid to developing countries.

The promotion of such cultural and scientific diplomacy calls for structures giving a stronger steer to the main participants in the programme (the *Institut français*, *CampusFrance*, the AEFE and the private sector within the framework of partnerships such as the Foreign Office business grant programme), an optimal level of co-funding in all sectors of cooperation with the creation of foundations and co-funded bilateral programmes, economies of scale and management control of the cultural institutions.

In total, taking part in the implementation of this programme are the 161 cooperation and cultural action services (*Scac*), the 132 cultural centres and Institutes, the thirty Centres for French Studies,[2] the 445

---

[2] The Centres for French Studies (CEF) merged with *EduFrance* spaces to become *CampusFrance* spaces in January 2007. They are one-stop shops for any student with a studying project in France and aim at facilitating all the administrative contacts.

(of the 920) *Alliances françaises* with agreements, and the twenty-seven research centres.

On 1 October 2010, the *Fondation Alliance française* signed a triennial convention with the Ministry of European and Foreign Affairs which envisages a convergence of the visual identities of the two public and private networks, the complementary nature of geographic locations and the increase in joint initiatives.

In education, the partnership with the *Mission laïque française* is also an important element of the network representing a 6.5 per cent budget share of the *Diplomatie culturelle et d'influence* programme (see Table 7.1). An agreement signed on 18 May 2010 with the Ministry of European and Foreign Affairs defines the strands of this partnership in which the *Mission* plays its full role. This organization, a non-profit association founded in 1902 and state approved in 1907, covers forty-seven countries and educates almost 44,000 students in 110 institutions around the world, in classes ranging from nursery to sixth form.

Cultural cooperation and the promotion of the French language, with a 10.5 per cent budget share, aims at developing the cultural and audiovisual industries, as well as the debate of ideas and the status of French as an international language as a tool for development in the francophone countries of the South, and the teaching of French in foreign education systems as well as in academic and professional training.

Global economic, social or environmental issues, with a 1.3 per cent budget share, call for better international coordination for sustainable development and in preparing for the United Nations Conference in Brazil in 2012 and also the negotiation of a global agreement following the political commitments of the Copenhagen Conference on Climate Change in 2009. These themes of better-regulated globalization were also on the agenda of the G8 and G20 meetings in 2011, under the presidency of France.

Attractiveness and research, with a 14.6 per cent share of the budget, aims at enhancing the academic attractions of France and at incorporating French research into the leading international networks.

Services to state education abroad are given 55.5 per cent of the budget for the *Agence française pour l'enseignement français à l'étranger*. This indicates clearly its importance for cultural, education and linguistic initiatives.

Expenses for staffing the *Diplomatie culturelle et d'influence* programme amount to 11.6 per cent of the 2011 budget.

## Management Control

There is a relation between these budget shares and the performance indicators retained in the evaluation of each activity within the programme of cultural and influence diplomacy, indicating in very practical terms the main criteria for each of the objectives in order of importance.

Thus, the number of site visits and the efficiency of the *Agence pour la diffusion de l'information technologique (Adit)*[3] site hosting the database produced by the scientific services, from the user's point of view, allow an evaluation of the knowledge bank of the services for science and technology.

### Objective 1: Responding to the Issues of Globalization

The two indicators are the average cost of one visit to the *Adit* site and the number of visitors to the site. The number of students enrolled in bilingual school sections, the number of those attending language classes in French cultural institutions and *Alliances françaises*, the number of student-hours of language classes in such, the number of examination candidates for certification in and tests of French, are a primary series of indicators allowing the evaluation of the influence of France in Europe and around the world.

### Objective 2: Strengthening the Influence of France in Europe and the World

The number of students enrolled on francophone courses must be complemented by information on the attractiveness of France for a foreign audience. Thus the percentage of foreign students passing the *baccalaureate* abroad and proceeding to higher education studies either in France or elsewhere through a joint French programme of academic cooperation, and the number of foreign students enrolled in French master's or doctoral programmes, are two essential indicators. The stimulation of the external

---

[3] Created in 1992, the *Agence pour la diffusion de l'information technologique* started as an *établissement publique à caractère industriel et commercial* (Epic) and became in 2003 a limited company wholly state-owned by the Ministère de l'Economie, des Finances et de l'Industrie. Its tasks are the collecting, collating and dissemination of international scientific and cultural information in support of the development of French commercial companies.

financial resources and the average cost per student to the state are two useful measures for the management of credits

*Objective 3: Improving Financial Control and Efficiency*
The same applies to the financial management of staff expenses, expatriate staff remuneration – grade-related salaries and weighting allowances, family income supplements and specific family payments, together with financing personnel according to local law and pay scales.

One sensitive issue, especially at a time of public policy reviews, is the staffing and levels of service and thus the determination of spending limits. The sustained decline in the number of full-time equivalent staff (FTEs) in diplomatic posts and education institutions often raises anxieties as to the functioning of the cultural and scientific network.

**Personnel and Recruitment Policies**

This function is somewhat delicate, in that it covers very diverse policies, training origins and career paths. There are three categories of personnel:

- First, career diplomats – secretaries or counsellors from Foreign Affairs who elect, for a given time, to hold a cultural or scientific position in an embassy or in the central administration.

- Second, permanent civil service personnel, who are posted, for a contractual period, from their home administration service to the *Ministère des Affaires étrangères et européennes* (MAEE) [Ministry of Foreign and European Affairs], from the *Ministère de l'Education nationale* or the *Ministère de l'Enseignement Supérieur et de la Recherche* or from such as the Culture, Finance or Agriculture Ministries.

- The third category comprises personnel recruited locally by the diplomatic staff.

In 2011, the 1,182 full-time equivalent places of the *Diplomatie culturelle et d'influence* programme consisted of 138 permanent staff or those with permanent contracts in central administration and sixty-six out in the network; 760 had fixed-term contracts or were international volunteers and 218 were locally recruited agents; there was no one from the military.

These staff members are an essential interface between the various players and the national and international organizations, state and private. It is of note that the third category of personnel, and international volunteers, are increasingly replacing those in the second category.

Choosing the right person for the job then becomes crucial, especially at times of budget restraint and a decrease in the number of posts on offer. The redeployment of finance and personnel can often lead to a limiting of choices for action in some priority areas according to country, due to static or declining resources.

The *Livre blanc sur la politique étrangère et européenne de la France 2008–2020*, under the presidency of Alain Juppé and Louis Schweitzer (July 2008), had clearly identified this trend:

> The human resource management of the MAEE is particularly difficult: the constraints and rigidities generally encountered in the civil service are made worse by the complexity engendered by the mobility and specific nature of diplomatic work. The turnover of personnel in the MAEE is one of the highest in the state institutions. The average duration of assignment is three years. [...] We must add to this the difficulties of expatriate life, often in conditions of doubtful security, and of family separation, which add to the constraints of an exciting but professionally demanding job, often difficult for personnel and families. Confronted with this situation, it is imperative that the specific nature of this occupation be recognized and that, at the highest level, clear strategic objectives should be defined in recruiting, training and career management.[4]

Thus, recognizing foreign-based occupations as a professional element of the civil service, developing specializations during a whole career, strengthening initial and continuing education, improving assignment policies and career management and devising an effective policy on human resources where local recruitment is required are the many operational objectives to be pursued to better manage the expatriate community.

---

[4] Alain Juppé and Louis Schweitzer, *La France et l'Europe dans le monde: livre blanc sur la politique étrangère et européenne de la France 2008–2020* (Paris: La Documentation française, 2008), pp. 138–9.

Table 7.1 *Budget of the 'foreign activities of the state' groupings, 2010–2011 (€ million)*

| Programme/Initiative | Authorized | | Allocated | |
|---|---|---|---|---|
| Heading number | 2010 | 2011 (draft) | 2010 | 2011 (draft) |
| 105 Action of France in Europe and the world | 1,732.2 | 1,801.4 | 1,702.1 | 1,814.4 |
| 185 Cultural and influence diplomacy | 768.8 | 757.6 | 769.6 | 757.6 |
| - *Network operations* | (45.9) | (49.4) | (45.9) | (49.4) |
| - *Cultural cooperation and the promotion of the French language* | (86.1) | (79.3) | (86.9 | (79.3) |
| - *Global economic, social or environmental issues* | (10.5) | (9.8) | (10.5) | (9.8) |
| - *Attractiveness and research* | (115.8) | (110.3) | (115.8)[1] | (110.3) |
| - *French foreign teaching agency* | (421.3) | (420.8) | (421.3) | (420.8) |
| - *Personnel expenses* | (89.2) | (88.1) | (892.0) | (88.1) |
| 151 French abroad and consular affairs | 325.5 | 343.2 | 325.7 | 343.2 |
| 332 French presidency of G8 and G20 | – | 60.0 | – | 50.0 |
| | 2,826.5 | 2,962.2 | 2,797.4 | 2,965.2 |

[1] Formerly the *Rayonnement culturel et scientifique*.

*Source*: Government budget documents.

# Conclusion

Between the Juppé and Schweitzer White Paper reasserting the necessity for a global cultural and scientific network[1] and the general review of public policies implying a reduction of activity, the cultural and scientific initiatives of France must be undertaken in a context of declining staff numbers and dwindling state finance.

France has set up a classification of its embassies, scheduled to have been finalized by the end of 2011. The premier category is 'embassies with extended roles', with a remit to cover the whole range of diplomatic activities, such as defence, culture, economy, security and sounding political alerts; a second category is 'with priority roles', which will be required to prioritize some activities, at the expense of others that will be allowed to lapse; a third category 'with specific powers' will result in a reduced French presence. This evolution will have consequences for the organization of work and of the services provided.

This context, which is not unique to France, specifies the priority areas and where to develop partnerships and co-funding, public and private. This evolution necessitates exploiting the synergies between ministries and state links with business and civil society. Notable is the role of the Foreign Office, the *Quai d'Orsay*, in partnership with the *Ministère de la Culture et de l'Education nationale* and the *Ministère de l'Enseignement supérieur et de la Recherche*, as stated by three French ambassadors, each a former general secretary to the *Quai d'Orsay* from 1998 to 2002:

[1] Alain Juppé and Louis Schweitzer, *La France et l'Europe dans le monde: livre blanc sur la politique étrangère et européenne de la France 2008–2020* (Paris: La Documentation française, 2008).

Having a strong Ministry of Foreign Affairs is now vital. The two former ministers, who have given their opinion, had each in turn tried to raise public awareness on this. The White Paper on French foreign policy, directed by Alain Juppé and Louis Schweitzer, already identified the paradox of having 'on one side a competitive world, fragmented, dangerous, and particularly exacting for our efforts abroad, and on the other side a Ministry of European and Foreign Affairs with ever diminishing resources'.[2]

The report on France and globalization submitted by Hubert Védrine to the French president underlined that 'France really needs a big ministry of World Affairs. It exists: it is the Ministry of Foreign Affairs. And if an umpteenth reform has to be made, then it must strengthen and reassert its interministerial role'.[3]

It is indeed always a question of improving the image of France[4] and developing the communication policies of the various operators and organizations in charge of foreign policy. The great projects of cultural and scientific cooperation discussed in this volume will have a real impact only if they are highlighted and evaluated in terms of the influence they may have on the countries or regions where they are implemented. The evaluation and impact of cultural and scientific policies are certainly vital at times of declining levels of public funding and the quest for new partnerships.

Christian Masset introduced the budget in the 2011 finance bill thus:

In accordance with the wishes of the members of the parliament, sums allocated for Programmes 185 and 209 have a revised presentation: from the former geographic approach, Programme 185 for the North and Programme 209 for the South, we switch to a logic of strategy, better distinguishing cultural and influence initiatives on the one hand and solidarity with developing countries on the other. This distinction, however, has no effect on staff costs, since agents frequently operate for both programmes. At present, we are developing new tools, under the

[2] François Scheer, Bertrand Dufourcq and Loïc Hennekinne, 'Le Quai, outil vital d'une diplomatie efficace', *Le Monde*, 25 August 2010.

[3] Hubert Védrine, 'Rapport pour le Président de la République sur la France et la mondialisation' (September 2007), p. 59.

[4] According to Bernard Plasait, in *Améliorer l'image de la France* (Paris: Editions des Journaux Officiels, 2010).

law of 27 July 2010 on the foreign activities of the state, conforming as closely as possible to the means and objectives of the conventions with the operators, and this budget is the first application of the new triennial planning law for 2010–2013. Last, our action must take into account the prime minister's direction to reduce public deficits: the department has been asked to cut its expenses by 10 per cent within three years, and by 5 per cent for 2011.

Programme 185 benefits from the continuation of extra funding of €20 million to relaunch foreign cultural initiatives, the maintenance of student grants [...] for the support to new operators of the foreign activities of the state and for the ring-fencing of AEFE funds for three years. [...] The operator will in fact redistribute funding between posts and also the *Alliances françaises*.[5]

The *Solidarité à l'égard des pays en voie de développement* programme keeps its full funding allocation. State aid for development is maintained, despite the necessity of reducing public spending and bilateral cooperation benefits from an adjustment from 31 per cent to 35 per cent, owing to a reduction of France's participation in the European Development Fund. Moreover, the 'grants and projects' initiative progresses well, with specific measures for Afghanistan, Haiti and Pakistan. Last, it must be stressed that support to non-governmental organizations is maintained.

The programme for the 2011 French presidency of the G20 and G8 summits was funded over two years. Indeed, France is the first country to preside over both summits simultaneously, at a time when the conscience of international cooperation and the rise of national ambitions go hand in hand, when we must find a multipolar mode of governance with key words such as regulation, development and influence.

This is the general framework for the development of France's cultural and scientific initiatives. It benefits from autonomy in the conception and implementation of projects within the sectors concerned, and from relating to global issues which are those of French diplomacy. This structure calls for effective cooperation with other ministries and organizations, particularly for science and technology, a major issue of influence with economic implications.

The sustainability of the funding of new agencies asked to perform public service duties is vital and the same applies to the imperative

---

[5] See <www.senat.fr/rap/a10-112-2/a10-112-211.html>.

consultation between ministries so as to optimize the means to mutual benefit and create the conditions for dynamic and responsive governance. This is a strength of other European countries' agencies, not to overlook France's exceptionally strong relations with the diplomatic services in the embassies and consulates.

The scope of cultural and scientific activity is extremely broad and implies a concerted effort on the part of the various players: cooperation and cultural activity services, services for science and technology, cultural centres and *Instituts français*, *Alliances françaises* and French education institutions. The growing specialization of the different functions is a challenge for France to return to a more collective way of working so that the country can offer its foreign partners a more concerted and coherent programme of action, in accord with the projects for cooperation.

# Index

Printed and bound by CPI Group (UK) Ltd, Croydon, CR0 4YY

13/04/2025

14656594-0005